# JOURNAL OF LEGAL PLURAL
## and Unofficial Law

**NUMBER 50 / 2004**

CONTENTS

**Bibliographic information published by Die Deutsche Bibliothek**
Die Deutsche Bibliothek lists this publication in the Deutsche
Nationalbibliografie; detailed bibliographic data are available in the
Internet at http://dnb.ddb.de.

ISSN 0732-9113
ISBN 3-8258-9355-3



**A catalogue record for this book is available from the British Library**



© LIT VERLAG Berlin 2006
Auslieferung/Verlagskontakt:
Grevener Str./Fresnostr. 2   48159 Münster
Tel. +49 (0)251–62 03 20   Fax +49 (0)251–23 19 72
e-Mail: lit@lit-verlag.de   http://www.lit-verlag.de

Distributed in the UK by: Global Book Marketing, 99B Wallis Rd, London, E9 5LN
Phone: +44 (0) 20 8533 5800 – Fax: +44 (0) 1600 775 663
http://www.centralbooks.co.uk/acatalog/search.html

Distributed in North America by:

Transaction Publishers
New Brunswick (U.S.A.) and London (U.K.)

Transaction Publishers
Rutgers University
35 Berrue Circle
Piscataway, NJ 08854

Phone: +1 (732) 445 - 2280
Fax: + 1 (732) 445 - 3138
for orders (U. S. only):
toll free (888) 999 - 6778
e-mail:
orders@transactionspub.com

# JOURNAL OF LEGAL PLURALISM
## and Unofficial Law

### POLICY

The Journal of Legal Pluralism and Unofficial Law (JLP) is a refereed, independent, inter-disciplinary, international journal devoted to scholarly writing, documentation, information on current developments, and communications about all aspects of legal pluralism and unofficial law anywhere in the world and at any time. Issues 1-18 bear the name *African Law Studies*.

### MANUSCRIPTS

Manuscripts for the Journal of Legal Pluralism should be submitted to the editor-in-chief:
Gordon R. Woodman
School of Law, University of Birmingham
Edgbaston, Birmingham B15 2TT
United Kingdom
Fax: (+ 44) (0)121 414 3585
Email: G.R.Woodman@bham.ac.uk
or to one of the associate editors. Unless the editors are otherwise informed, submission of a manuscript implies the undertaking that it is not currently being considered by another journal and that if accepted it will be available for publication.

Manuscripts must conform to the style and other instructions contained in the JLP 'style sheet' (printed at the end of nr. 39 and to be found on the JLP web site under the title 'Author guidelines'), and should generally be submitted in electronic form.

### SUBSCRIPTIONS

Subscriptions to the Journal of Legal Pluralism are currently €27.00 for individuals and €52.50 for institutions. A subscription consists of two numbers, each of approximately 200 pages. From nr. 49 (2004) the Journal has been published by LIT Verlag, Münster-Hamburg-Berlin-Vienna-London, whose address for orders is Grevener St./Fresnostr.2, D-48159 Münster, Germany, Fax (+49) (0)251 23 19 72, vertrieb@lit-verlag.de.

Back numbers of African Law Studies and the Journal of Legal Pluralism to nr. 48 are available from William S. Hein & Co., Inc., 1285 Main Street, Buffalo, New York 14209-1987, USA..

### INDEXES AND DATABASES

Articles appearing in the Journal of Legal Pluralism are indexed in the principal legal and social science indexes and online data-bases. The full text of all articles published more than two years previously will be available from the end of 2005 on databases maintained by the Journal of Legal Pluralism at www.jlp.bham.ac.uk, and by HeinOnLine at www.heinonline.org/front/front-index

### CITATION

The Journal of Legal Pluralism and Unofficial Law should be cited as: *Journal of Legal Pluralism*.

# CONTENTS

# CONTENTS

BOOK REVIEW

# FROM THE EDITORS

This number of the *Journal of Legal Pluralism* contains, as always, articles about varied aspects of diverse societies. Richard Crook writes about the use of state courts in Ghana; Arnaldo Godoy reflects on general aspects of the Brazilian experience of legal pluralism; Bishnu Upreti examines the control between different bodies of law of natural resources in Nepal; Kathryn Fulton considers socio-economic developments in an Alaskan village also caught between two laws representing dramatically different views of the good society. Three articles are about aspects of law in India, but they discuss issues which have little else in common except that they are manifested within the national boundaries of that large and complex country: Julia Eckert is concerned with the interaction between state law and the newly developed normative order of a political party in a large city; Karine Bates with an instance of national legislation which attempts to change social practice in inheritance law, with strong implications for gender issues; and Pampa Mukherjee with legal control of the natural resource of forests in Uttranchal state. Making another contrast, Yüksel Sezgin does not report on empirical research but proposes a mode of analysing instances of legal pluralism which enables a quantification of degrees of plurality, and which is seen as applicable to every legal arena in the world.

Most of these articles were first presented, often in a form which has since undergone considerable revision, at meetings of the Commission on Folk Law and Legal Pluralism. More such papers may be selected for the next issue of the *Journal*. The Commission will hold its 15th international congress in Depok, West Java, Indonesia, from 29 June to 2 July 2006, with the theme "Law, Power and Culture: Transnational, National and Local Processes in the Context of Legal Pluralism". The Commission will also take part in the congress of its parent body, the International Union of Anthropological and Ethnological Sciences, in Kunming, China in 2008. Details of these and all other activities of the Commission may be found on its website at http://www.unb.ca/cflp/.

Gordon Woodman

# ABSTRACTS OF ARTICLES

## ACCESS TO JUSTICE AND LAND DISPUTES IN GHANA'S STATE COURTS: THE LITIGANTS' PERSPECTIVE

Richard C. Crook

The majority of land in Ghana is still held under a diversity of customary tenures, embedded in family, community and chiefly institutions; but land disputes may be adjudicated in a variety of institutions: informal arbitrations and family tribunals, chiefs' courts, quasi-legal state agencies and the formal state courts. Current debates on how to protect the land rights of the majority of customary land holders revolve around the respective merits of customary and non-state regulation (said to be accessible, flexible and socially embedded), and state systems, which are said to offer more certainty, impartiality and non-discriminatory codes and procedures. In Ghana, however, customary and state legal codes have been integrated for some time, and the state courts, which are frequently used as first instance adjudicators, apply customary rules. Does this mean that in Ghana the merits of customary law can be combined with the certainty and enforceability of state court dispute settlement?

Based primarily on survey and interview data, the research analyses how litigants in three selected state courts perceived the experience of taking their land cases to court. It was found that, in spite of the problems and delays associated with the state courts, there was a very strong demand for authoritative and enforceable remedies which only the state could provide. It was also found that the justice offered by the state courts was not as alien or inappropriate as commonly supposed. Particularly in the Magistrates Court, judges were well respected and their procedures seen as sufficiently flexible and user-friendly. Moreover, the extreme reluctance to entertain out-of- court settlements casts doubt on the notion that proposals to move to more use of ADRs will be successful if they fail to offer equivalent authority, fairness and enforceability.

# URBAN GOVERNANCE AND EMERGENT FORMS OF LEGAL PLURALISM IN MUMBAI

Julia Eckert

The little discussed forms of legal pluralism that emerge within the effective administration of justice and entitlements by state and non-state agencies have long determined the operative legal order of (urban) India. They are considered here in relation to the 'selective state', characterised by the formal and informal devolution of judicial competences of the state to alternative organisations. The merger of devolution and appropriation gives rise to new forms of legal pluralism, illustrated in Mumbai by the *Shiv Sena*, a regional political party of the Hindu Right.

The *Shiv Sena* has established local party offices, the *Shakhas*, in every part of Mumbai as well as in most towns and villages of the state of Maharashtra. The *Shakhas* offer numerous local services, performing distributive and productive tasks which involve the organisation of allocation. The *Shiv Sena* also through the *Shakhas* explicitly takes on regulatory functions in many matters, most clearly in their administration of local disputes. An informal system of 'courts' within the *Shakhas* deals with disputes relating to everyday living in the city, including civil as well as criminal matters, and often also administrative regulation. Judgments are swiftly enforced, by violence if necessary. Rulings are said to be guided by 'common sense', this notion involving implicitly the *Shiv Sena*'s notions of the proper order, but being also intricately linked to local social relations. The *Shiv Sena*'s courts are justified on grounds of accessibility and efficiency, supporting the party's general claim to fulfil state tasks better than the state itself. However, the operative legal order thus established is not hegemonic. It is constantly open to adaptations and changes that result from plural pressures and the competitive normative offers of various actors in the field of adjudication, and thus sways between phases of monopolisation and dominance and phases of pluralisation and adaptation. In the daily practice of the *Shiv Sena* issues such as those of women's rights are often dealt with in contradictory ways, differing from one *Shakha* to the other, as well as depending on the specific local constellation and demands.

The *Shiv Sena* has achieved a relatively high degree of institutional incorporation into state modes of governance. Its interpretations and enactments of law are (re-) introduced into the practices of state agencies, and its institutional integration with some state agencies is one of various degrees of cooperation and complementarity, and thus of mutual interdependence. The case of the *Shiv Sena* suggests a question as to the interaction between state and non-state legal orders. In studies of legal pluralism, while non-state legal orders are said to be semi-autonomous, state law is often treated as autonomous, as shaping but not as being shaped. In Mumbai state law is constitutive of the rules of the game, but seems also to be fundamentally transformed by the productions of legal order in the interactions of various actors involved in the administration of law and order, resulting in what is a relatively integrated operative legal order. The case sheds light on the complex matters of the use and transformation of law and the precariousness of power relations. It suggests that in India the emergence of the dominance of local governance by organisations like the *Shiv Sena*, ensues from a merger of cunning devolution by the state and forceful appropriation by local organisations.

# GLOBALIZATION, STATE LAW AND LEGAL PLURALISM IN BRAZIL

Arnaldo Moraes Godoy

Globalization has had an immense impact on traditional political concepts such as sovereignty. This paper argues that the modern nation-state is no longer the principal form of political rule across the globe and that legal pluralism could be on the rise. In South America, as globalization diminishes the size and burdens of traditional nation-states, legal pluralism seems to reappear in order to fill normative spaces that are left empty. This seems to happen, thanks to the new shape of a minimal state, as a result of a new world order. Legal pluralism can also represent a cluster of alternatives against the normative destruction that globalization has effected in the world's legal cultures. Conflict between institutions in a worldwide trade of cultural values suggests the victory of the stronger. A sort of social Darwinism has been in operation and the weakest partners in today's globalized world are facing the implementation of new forms of conflict compositions. Because there is a weak and minimal state present in most of South America today, traditional sources of power have been the objects of popular distrust. As one can easily find out in Brazil's forensic and non-forensic realms, many different legal experiences have been unfolding. Several patterns of non-traditional jurisdiction, alternative dispute resolution in the field of labor law, neighborhood councils to prevent crime, lay arbitrators, etc. suggest there is something new in the air. The declining authority of the state has implications for the ordinary citizen, who wants options to solve the problems under which he or she labors. The paper reveals an unexpected relationship between globalization and legal pluralism in South America, presenting a case study in Brazil. It shows that instead of creating a world shaped by sameness, globalization can be responsible for the empowerment of local institutions. So there is a chance of rescue from an imminent tragedy of cultural loss that we are all about to face in less developed countries.

# RELATIONSHIPS BETWEEN RESOURCE GOVERNANCE AND RESOURCE CONFLICT: NEPALESE EXPERIENCES

Bishnu Upreti

This paper highlights the relationships between resource rights, governance practices and conflict in Nepal. The discussion is focused on policies, strategies, laws and regulations, and decisions and actual governing practices in natural resources. The good governance framework is used as a conceptual basis to analyse the relationships. This framework is for the purpose of this paper consensus oriented, participatory, guided by the rule of law, effective and efficient, accountable and transparent, responsive, equitable and inclusive. Within this framework, the paper examines the role of resource governance in creating or minimising scarcity and conflict in Nepal. It is based on my current research project on 'livelihood security, environmental security and conflict mitigation' in Nepal. It highlights power relations, feelings of injustice, mistrust, the intervention of new technologies, contradiction between customary practices and statutory laws as sources of research. Resource conflicts produce both positive and negative consequences and alter existing social relations, as they induce change in resource management regimes, policy process, livelihood strategies, land use patterns, gender relations, power structures, and individual and collective behaviour. This paper also establishes the linkages between resource conflict and the ongoing Maoist insurgency in Nepal.

JOURNAL OF LEGAL PLURALISM
2004 – nr.50

# THEORIZING FORMAL PLURALISM: QUANTIFICATION OF LEGAL PLURALISM FOR SPATIO-TEMPORAL ANALYSIS

Yüksel Sezgin

The different types of legal pluralism have been extensively studied by many anthropologists and legal scholars. But what about the intensity or degree of pluralism? Does this always stay the same or does it ever change over time? Legal pluralism is the reflection of complex human interactions in our normative universe. It changes as a society evolves. With these changes in its form and structure, the degree of plurality also changes. As a result, societies constantly become 'more' or 'less' pluralistic as they evolve. In order to capture these spatio-temporal variations in degrees of legal pluralism, this paper aims to introduce a simple technique of quantification which measures the differing degrees of legal pluralism both over time and across localities. The major benefit of quantification will be to enable those students of legal pluralism who wish to undertake more macro-sociological and cross-national analyses to reach some theoretical generalizations and compare different legal systems at a higher level of abstraction. Along the same lines, the paper also offers a number of theoretical, methodological and ontological novelties to better facilitate a diachronic analysis of legal pluralism.

# THE HINDU SUCCESSION ACT: ONE LAW, PLURAL IDENTITIES

Karine Bates

A broad definition of law manifests itself in various ways: it legitimates certain visions of social order, it determines relations between individuals and groups, and it manipulates cultural understandings and discourses over various concepts of rights - and duties. In India, the *Hindu Succession Rights Act (HSA)* of 1956 allows the wife and daughters, along with the sons of the deceased senior male, to claim an equal share in familial property. By giving inheritance rights to daughters and widows, not only to sons, this Act proposes a radically different organization of the ideal household, commonly referred to as the 'Indian joint family'. The Act initiates a transformation of Hindu women's status through their rights to property, which implies the transformation of women's rights and duties in India. It also affects men's access to natal property and modifies brother-sister relationships. Moreover, it redefines some religious categories. Firstly, under this Act the category 'Hindu' includes Hindu, Buddhist, Jain or Sikh. Secondly, it regulates the multiple religious and inheritance practices that still exist in different parts of India.

Like other national laws concerning the personal rights of the Hindu population, the *HSA* is the result of a compromise between different legal traditions such as various Hindu schools of law, British common law and the western philosophy underlying the concept of equality. The long debate over personal laws that took place in the 1950s led Indian legislators to envisage a new 'social order' in their laws, which would become potential agents of social change. But such legislative initiatives are not sufficient because their success depends on tribunals' reactions and their capacity and desire to elaborate a new jurisprudence. In addition, innovative legal cases depend on people's knowledge of the law and their desire to use it instead of other forms of conflict resolution. Drawing on observations made during an extensive fieldwork period in a rural community and case studies in Pune tribunals, this paper shows that women know that they have some rights to their fathers' and husbands' property. However, for various reasons, they do not see any advantage in claiming those rights. Women often find it difficult to reconcile claiming rights with their duties as daughters or daughters-in-law and the social restrictions associated with widowhood. This socio-legal ethnography of women's succession rights in the state of Maharashtra contributes to the understanding of the dynamics of social cohesion in an environment where legal pluralism offers plural sources of identity definition and transformation.

# WHEN LEGAL PROCEDURALISM CONFUSES THE VALUES OF LEADERSHIP: 'OFFICIAL' AND 'UNOFFICIAL' LAW IN A TLINGIT COMMUNITY

Kathryn Fulton

In 1914 a small Alaska Tlingit village received permission from the United States Customs agent to form a local city government. One Tlingit man recorded his memories of the formal ceremony "to abolish the old customs of government and adopt the new government introduced by the Americans, a radical decision at that time" (Jackson 2002). He remembered the new mayor's words, that Keex' Kwaan (not its official name),

...has been like a small child. In the white man's way of living, we can only crawl. We're not prepared; we have no education. So it was like a little child that could crawl, but now with our self government (Keex' Kwaan) is going to get on its feet, and we'll begin to walk .... The white man's law went beyond the authority of the Tlingit chiefs, so some of them see it that there was no necessity for chiefs anymore. (Jackson 2002)

Today, the contradictions, inconsistencies and discrepancies between an 'adopted' Euro-American political system, which professes equal access to political representation, and older Tlingit practices and values have produced a social and legal paradox. The ironic result in Keex' Kwaan has largely been government polarization and disenfranchisement. Fernandez and Huber (2001: 4) observed that "irony can be expected in situations of unequal power when discourses, interests or culture clash." In this case, the US colonizer's ideological over-confidence, that its laws and political and economic processes are 'best for all', has led to a 'predicament of irony' which makes economic problem-solving difficult in Keex' Kwaan.

# COMMUNITY RIGHTS AND STATUTORY LAWS: POLITICS OF FOREST USE IN UTTRANCHAL HIMALYAS

Pampa Mukherjee

In the last two decades while 'decentralized governance' and 'participation' have become buzz words among policy planners and bureaucrats, in actual practice communities are being pushed to the margins. National and state laws still define the major concerns of Indian society and polity. The present paper aims to highlight the dominance of statutory laws over local self-governing institutions and how community space is constricted in the name of participatory governance. It argues that communities are treated as mere beneficiaries rather than as active partners. It also highlights the fact that the introduction of New Joint Forest Management in 1996 has overridden the customary claims of communities on forests practiced over decades. Further, it shows how boundaries and fences have become sites of anxiety, creating artificial enclaves and plots, and in the process excluding communities from their rightful access to resources

# ABOUT THE CONTRIBUTORS

Karine BATES completed an undergraduate degree in civil and common law, and then pursued graduate degree studies in legal anthropology. She obtained a Ph.D. degree from McGill University, Canada, in 2005 for a thesis entitled "Women's Property Rights and Access to Justice in India: A Socio-Legal Ethnography of Widowhood and Inheritance Practices in Maharashtra." At the same university, she created an undergraduate level course in Legal Anthropology which she taught in 2004. She is now a Post-Doctoral Scholar at the Department of Anthropology, University of Montreal, Canada. She holds a scholarship from the *Fonds Québécois de la recherche sur la société et la culture* for the purpose of deepening the analysis of access to justice in India, in part through a comparison between Maharashtra and Kerala.

Richard C. CROOK is Emeka Anyaoku Professor of Commonwealth Studies at the Institute of Commonwealth Studies, School of Advanced Studies, University of London. He holds a Ph.D. in Government from the London School of Economics and Political Science. He has spent his working life conducting research on and teaching about the politics and government of developing countries, especially in West Africa and South Asia. He has held positions at the Department of Politics, University of Glasgow, Britain, the Centre of West African Studies, University of Birmingham, Britain, and the Institute of Development Studies, University of Sussex, Britain. He has published extensively on local politics and decentralisation, state and civil society relations, and administrative performance. Among his more recent publications are: (with James Manor) *Democracy and Decentralisation in West African and South Asia: Participation, Accountability and Performance.* Cambridge University Press, 1998; (with Alan Sturla Sverrisson) *Decentralisation and Poverty Alleviation in Developing Countries: A Comparative Analysis or, Is West Bengal Unique?* Brighton: Institute of Development Studies, 2001.

Julia ECKERT studied Political Science, Sociology and Social Anthropology at the Albert Ludwigs University in Freiburg, Germany, and the Free University Berlin. Her first field research was carried out in Pakistan in 1991 and concerned the changing political structures among Afghan refugees in the refugee camps in Peshawar and Quetta. Subsequently she undertook field research in Uzbekistan, publishing a monograph *Das unabhängige Usbekistan auf dem Weg von Marx zu Timur [Independent Uzbekistan on the route from Marx to Timur].* Munster: LIT Verlag, 1994. In 1995 she joined the Institute for International Educational Research

(DIPF) in Frankfurt am Main. 1997 she started her Ph.D. research in India on the *Shiv Sena* movement. She was subsequently a lecturer at the Institute for Social Anthropology, Free University Berlin, and at the Institute for Social Sciences, Humboldt University Berlin, before joining the Project Group on Legal Pluralism at the Max Planck Institute for Social Anthropology, Halle, Germany as a senior research fellow in May 2001. Her most recent book publications are: *"The Charisma of Direct Action: Power, Politics and the Shivsena.* Delhi: Oxford University Press, 2003; *Partizipation und die Politik der Gewalt; Hindunationalismus und Demokratie in Indien [Participation and the Politics of Violence: Hindu Naitonalism and Democracy in Indai].* Baden-Baden: Nomos, 2004.

Kathryn FULTON, born in Idaho, USA, is a Faculty Fellow in the Department of Anthropology, Colby College, Waterville, Maine, USA. She is a PhD candidate, at the University of Oregon, USA. Her current research areas include fishing villages in southeast Alaska, and she has conducted research among ranchers in the US Midwest. An environmental anthropologist, her research and theoretical interests include: Native Americans, Northwest Coast Tlingits, environment, space/place, gender, community studies, fisheries/fishers, forests/forest workers, prairies/ranchers, government policy, narrative discourse analysis, participant action research methodology and applied anthropology. She has presented numerous conference papers on her research.

Arnaldo Moraes GODOY is a Professor at the Pontifical Catholic University of the State of Paraná, Brazil. He has published *Direito e Historia: Uma Relacao Equivocada [Law and History: An Equivocal Relationship]*, 2003.

Pampa MUKHERJEE is a Senior Lecturer at the Department of Political Science, Punjab University, Chandigarh, India. She completed her Masters, M.Phil and doctoral studies at the Centre for Political Studies, Jawaharlal Nehru University, Delhi. She teaches and does research on development politics, Natural Resource Management, Gender and politics, and has published in these areas. She has done detailed work on Common Property Resources particularly in the hilly regions of North India. She has been involved with number of national and International projects in these areas and presently working on a book *Common, Communities and Conservation: Politics of Forest Use in Uttranchal.*

Yüksel SEZGIN is a Ph.D. candidate in Political Science at the University of Washington, Seattle, USA. He holds an MA in Near and Middle Eastern Studies from the School of Oriental and African Studies, University of London, and the

Hebrew University of Jerusalem. His recent publications include 'A political account for legal confrontation between state and society: the case of Israeli legal pluralism.' Pp. 199-235 in Austin Sarat & Patricia Ewick (eds.), *Studies in Law, Politics, and Society* Vol. 32, 2004,

Bishnu Raj UPRETI gained a Ph.D. in conflict management from Wageningen University, The Netherlands, in 2001. He is engaged in conflict analysis, conflict management, and research related to peace building. During his 24 years of professional experience he has taught and conducted research at the Universities of London and Surrey, Britain, and has worked in international organisations (including UNDP, SDC, IDRC, IUCN, SNV, UMN) as a member of the professional staff and as consultant. He has also spent some years in the service of the government of Nepal as an assistant agricultural economist. He has published four books on conflict management and more than 100 articles in journals, magazines and edited books. He had coordinated a Nepal chapter of the regional research project on 'Livelihood and Environmental Security and Conflict Mitigation', which is being conducted in Bangladesh, India, Nepal, and Pakistan. Currently he directs a National Peace Research Institute and Resource Centre, Swiss National Centre of Competence in Research (NCCR)-North-South South Asia Coordination Office, SDC Complex, Ekantakuna, Jawalakhel, GPO Box 910, Kathmandu, Nepal, e-mail: bupreti@nccr.wlink.com.np.

# ACCESS TO JUSTICE AND LAND DISPUTES IN GHANA'S STATE COURTS: THE LITIGANTS' PERSPECTIVE[1]

Richard C. Crook

## 1. Regulation of Land Disputes in Ghana: Legal Pluralism and State vs. 'Non-State' Dispute Settlement Institutions

In Ghana, as in the West African region generally, contestation over land is particularly acute, and seems likely to intensify. The pressures of population growth, cash-crop led marketisation, large scale migration, and rapid urbanisation have produced increased competition and land scarcity, and increasingly politicised conflict over land (IIED 1999). Some of these conflicts - host communities vs. migrants, inter-communal, inter-generational, gender-based - reflect the embeddedness of land laws in local power structures and social group membership. Others are linked to the role of the state, either through its articulation with local regimes or through state attempts directly to control land;

[1] I am very grateful to the British Department for International Development (DFID) which has funded this research. All the views expressed here are those of the author alone and should not be taken to represent those of DFID. I am also grateful to Jarrod Lovett of the Institute of Development Studies, University of Sussex, who carried out the SPSS coding and data analysis of the surveys. An earlier version of this paper first appeared as an IDS Working Paper (January 2005), and I am grateful to the IDS (Sussex) for permission to use this material.

everywhere, these developments are deepening the marginalisation and exclusion of poor and vulnerable groups.

'Land regulation' regimes in such situations have a crucial impact on livelihood decisions concerning crop strategies, labour usage, and survival strategies in the city (DFID 2000). Although Ghana shares with other African countries a situation characterised by high levels of legal pluralism, its particular history, both pre-colonial and colonial, has produced a set of deeply rooted, local social institutions of land regulation which have always been more strongly supported by the state than in many other African states. During the colonial period British policies of Indirect Rule and policies for the regulation of land exploitation led to the incorporation of local or 'customary' laws into a unified common law system, through the institution of Native Courts (Crook 1986; Allott 1957; Crook 2001; Woodman 1996 and 2001). Legal reforms in Ghana since 1986 have incorporated all forms of land tenure, including customary forms, into a single statutory and common law framework, and subjected transfers to both title registration and centralised regulation by a national Lands Commission. But this attempted centralisation and integration of different kinds of regulation has so far proved ineffective, and traditional institutions remain strong (Kasanga et al. 1996; Kasanga and Kotey 2001). Ghana's National Land Policy, published in 1999, now seeks, amongst other things, to harmonise the legal and regulatory framework for land administration through law reform, establishment of special land courts and strengthened customary land authorities, and comprehensive mapping and registration of land holdings and land rights, both customary and modern (Ghana 1999).[2]

In this context, a key question which the legal and institutional reform process must address is how to develop judicial and regulatory institutions which will be effective in reducing or managing growing conflict over land, and protecting land rights, particularly of the rural and urban poor.

Current debates in the literature revolve around two main themes: first, should customary and other non-state land regimes be supported because of their inherent flexibility, social embeddedness and accessibility, or should it be concluded that they in fact facilitate 'legal rightlessness' of the poor as against the state and

---

[2] The policy is being implemented by the Land Administration Project Unit (LAPU) in the Ministry of Lands and Forestry.

locally inequitable power structures? (Berry 1993, 1997; Basset and Crummey 1993; Chauveau 1997; *contra* Chanock 1991; Ruf 1985; Léonard 1997).

Second, does the plurality of legal orders offer useful choices for the ordinary citizen ('forum shopping') (Benda-Beckmann, Keebet von 1991; Vanderlinden 1989; Griffiths 1986) or does it produce a general ambiguity, lack of enforceability and lack of protection for land rights, particularly for those who lack power in the urban areas (Farvacque and McAuslan 1992; Kasanga et al. 1996; van Leeuwen and van Steekelenburg 1995; Dembele 1997; Larbi et al., 2003)? Indeed, the debate over the problems involved in encouraging local, customary dispute resolution institutions and ADRs (Alternative Dispute Resolution systems) suggests for some commentators that the best way forward is in fact to strengthen the role of state courts and regulatory agencies within a reformed and more integrated system (Anderson 2003; Debroy 2000; Kees van Donge 1999; Nader 1979 and 2001; Maxwell et al. 1999).

In our research[3] on the institutions which regulate access to and dispute over land rights we therefore decided to pay as much attention to the state courts, in their capacity as regulators of land disputes, as to 'non-state' (informal) and customary dispute settlement mechanisms.

The state courts in Ghana, as provided under the 1992 Constitution and the Courts Act, 1993 (Act 459) continue to form a crucial element in the land regulation system - indeed some might say they are the most important. They are constitutionally endowed with the power to apply all the rules of law recognised in Ghana, whether customary, common law or statute, and are resorted to by very large numbers of litigants who wish to see an authoritative settlement of their case. Yet, as is well known, the state courts, particularly the courts of first instance – District Courts, formerly Community Tribunals and popularly known as Magistrates' Courts, and High Courts - have been in a state of crisis for some years, insofar as they are overwhelmed with the large volume of land cases, few of

---

[3] This article is drawn from work which forms part of a larger comparative project on 'Legal institutions and the protection of land rights in Ghana and Cote d'Ivoire', funded by DFID (UK), in collaboration with Professor Simplice Affou of IRD, Abidjan, CI, and Dr Daniel Hammond of the Department of Land Economy, Kwame Nkrumah University of Science and Technology, Kumasi, Ghana together with a team of researchers.

which can be heard or settled within a reasonable time. There is therefore an urgent need to think about ways in which the court system can be helped to provide a more effective judicial service for the land sector.

This article is based primarily on survey research which examined the functioning of selected state courts, focussing primarily on how they are perceived and experienced by those who use them: - litigants in land cases. How effective do people find these courts? Are they seen as capable of protecting land rights, do they produce results which are acceptable or legitimate in the eyes of the parties themselves, and how far can they contribute to resolving or mitigating the levels of conflict associated with access to, use of and disposal of land in Ghana?

Courts were selected courts from three case-study areas:

> 1. The Community Tribunal (now Magistrate's Court) in Goaso, which is the District Assembly capital of Asunafo rural district, an area of cash crop agriculture (mainly cocoa) with large migrant communities.

> 2. The High Court of Kumasi, which serves primarily an urban or peri-urban area characterised by marketisation, severe competition and conflict among statutory, traditional and 'informal' ( illegal) systems of land regulation. There are six judges sitting in the Kumasi High Court.

> 3. The High Court of Wa (Upper West Region) which serves an area where there is a low degree of marketisation, no perceived land shortage and land is allocated at low cost according to local customs. There are very few land disputes, but those that are emerging are linked to the peri-urban growth of this Regional capital.

The research was designed to address three fairly simple sets of questions:

> 1. Why do people go to Court, as opposed to other forms of dispute settlement institution? (What do they want or expect from the court process? Do they always want a full trial and judgment?)

2. What are their experiences of the litigation process? How 'user friendly' is it, how inclusive and acceptable is it to those who use it?

3. Are there ways in which the service can be improved?

In order to answer these questions we adopted a methodology which begins with the users themselves, and asks them directly about their experiences. We therefore carried out a targeted or purposive survey of 243 land case litigants in the relevant courts, randomly selected over a specified time period. This is unique data in that it is probably the first such survey in the history of research into the Ghanaian legal system. We also interviewed the providers of the judicial service - judges, lawyers, court officials - and observed court proceedings over the same time period.

## 2. The Court System: Background to the Current Situation

The current court system in Ghana was set up by the Courts Act, 1993, and consists of the superior Courts of Judicature - the Supreme Court, the Court of Appeal, the High Court and the Regional Tribunals - and the lower courts. The High Courts in each Region are both first instance courts for all civil and criminal matters, and exercise supervisory jurisdiction over the lower courts - Circuit Courts and Magistrates' Courts. Under the 1993 legislation the lowest court (at District level) was called a Community Tribunal, and incorporated a lay panel of community assessors sitting with a legally qualified magistrate. These were abolished by Executive Instrument in 2002 and reverted to being Magistrates' Courts under a single legally qualified judge. (The Tribunals were a legacy of the PNDC 'revolutionary' era which were incorporated into the main legal system in the 1993 legislation and served as a form of special criminal court at the Circuit and Regional levels) (Gocking 2000). Since 1993 the Fast Track High Courts have also been added to the system; these do not differ in their jurisdiction or composition, but only in their procedures (although there has been legal challenge to their 'constitutionality').

The Magistrate's Court is the lowest level of civil court which hears land cases; until 2002, it was limited to cases involving property not exceeding five million cedis (¢5m, approximately GB£300 at current rates) in value. This meant that they were the main first instance courts in the rural districts, but in the urban areas

Draft figures for the Accra Central Registry present a similar picture; according to Mrs Justice Wood, rates of settlement for land cases over the 1998 - 2001 period fell from 4.2% to 2.6%, and the average minimum time for a litigant who goes through all the levels of the appellate system is between three and five years - but could easily be as much as 15 years.

Although no break down of cases in the District or Magistrates' Courts is available, the number of civil cases dealt with and pending is even more overwhelming. As in the High Court, the number of new cases coming in each year far exceeds the rate of settlement. In 2003-4, the Magistrates' Courts nationally had 59, 031 cases before them, of which 71% were new cases that year. Of that total, 23, 351 (40%) were settled. In Ashanti the equivalent figures were 10, 293 total cases, of which 65% were new, and the number of cases settled was 4230 (41%) (Ghana, 2004).

The 'real cause' of this backlog is of course the subject of a national debate; on the one hand, it is argued that the problem is a 'demand side' one - it is said that Ghanaians are too ready to bring cases without exploring other methods first, that they are too litigious and pursue cases unnecessarily, or that the land tenure and land administration systems themselves are so ambiguous and confusing that they automatically generate 'excessive conflict'. On the other hand, many commentators argue that the problem is supply side - the courts ought to be able to cope with whatever is brought before them but they lack capacity or efficiency in some way. The idea that levels of litigation are 'excessive' is of course difficult to judge - excessive in relation to what standard? Clearly the fact that thousands of people feel impelled to move from informal dispute to formal court action reflects a social and economic reality which cannot be wished away. One needs to ask, why is this happening?

## 3. Litigants in the Case Study Courts

Our intention in this study was to find out how the courts are used by citizens and how they view their experience of litigation. We therefore selected a sample of actual litigants in three courts: the Kumasi High Court, the Goaso Magistrate's Court and the Wa High Court. The sample was drawn by interviewing all those who attended court for a land case during the period December 2002 - April 2003. This produced a sample of 243 respondents: 186 in Kumasi, 47 in Goaso, and 10 in Wa. Very few people refused to be interviewed when approached. (The sample in Wa is very small because there were very few cases in Wa, but the respondents were included in the total survey anyway, although it must be borne in mind that the conclusions of the survey will apply predominantly to the two southern courts). We deliberately tried to select a balance of plaintiffs and defendants: 55.6% were plaintiffs and 44.4% defendants. The basic socio-economic characteristics of the litigants were as shown in the following tables.

Table 3.1: Litigants survey: sex of respondents

|  | Valid % |
|---|---|
| Male | 69.0 |
| Female | 31.0 |
| Total | 100.0 |

Table 3.2: Litigants survey: age of respondents

|  | Valid % |
|---|---|
| 40-64 | 52.7 |
| 65+ | 34.9 |
| 26-39 | 12.4 |
| Total | 100.0 |

Table 3.3: Litigants survey: educational level of respondents

|  | Valid % |
|---|---|
| Up to Standard 7/MSLC | 47.3 |
| None | 30.0 |
| Secondary/TTC | 16.5 |
| Post-secondary | 6.3 |
| Total | 100.0 |

Table 3.4: Litigants survey: occupation of respondents

|  | Valid % |
|---|---|
| Farmer | 52.1 |
| Trader, Worker, Artisan | 23.9 |
| Middle-class professional | 15.5 |
| Retired | 3.8 |
| Pastor | 2.1 |
| Unemployed, Student | 1.7 |
| Home maker | .8 |
| Total | 100.0 |

As can be seen, the litigants were predominantly (just over two-thirds) male, and, as might be expected, were all from the older age groups. They also had higher levels of education than for the Ghana population as a whole - although not excessively so, given that the modal group, nearly half of the sample, had only a Standard 7/ Middle School Leaving Certificate (MSLC) level. But gender and education (or the lack of it), were quite highly correlated; 60.6% of the women respondents had no education as compared to 16.6% of the men. In occupational terms, the respondents were surprisingly typical of the general population, especially given the predominance of the urban/peri-urban Kumasi respondents in the sample. The number in white collar or professional occupations - including quite low paid clerical jobs - was only 15.5%. The most important conclusion here is that the survey suggests that 'going to Court' is not purely for the rich, powerful or highly educated; a wide range of ordinary citizens use the Courts, including many uneducated women, although clearly they are mainly older citizens and it is more likely to be men rather than women who go to the Court, perhaps on behalf of family groups rather than purely for themselves.

## 4. Why do People go to Court?

Given the expense and the possible delay, what is it that finally motivates somebody with a land dispute to abandon - or by-pass - the wide variety of informal and traditional methods of dispute resolution available in Ghanaian society, and file a land suit in Court? It can safely be predicted that there is not one single reason, but that it is probably a combination of factors which underlies such a step.

In the first place, we asked whether it was to do with the nature of the dispute; what kinds of land dispute were appearing in the Courts? The survey provided a surprising answer: the largest single category of cases (over 52% of the total) involved family disputes of some kind, mainly inheritance disputes between different sides of a family, amongst children of the deceased or between the widow and the children, disputes over unauthorised disposition of family land by an individual family member, and property disputes between divorcees (Table 4.1, next page).[8] The common stereotypical view that it is double sales or unauthorised dispositions and boundary disputes - allegedly caused by lack of boundary definition and registration of ownership - which are clogging up the courts is clearly inaccurate. The latter kinds of cases accounted for only 12.8% of the total. Cases against the government or the Lands Commission were a tiny proportion, only 1.2%.

It would be wrong, of course, to suggest that the distribution of types of cause in this survey is somehow representative of the general causes of land disputes in the population as a whole. Our survey of the general population in selected villages in our case-study areas showed that, of village respondents who had experienced a dispute, 50% said their disputes concerned 'trespass' and disputes with neighbours. Only 26% concerned family or inheritance matters. This demonstrates the clear difference between the kinds of cases which villagers attempt to settle themselves, and those which are more likely to end up in court. It is family disputes which are the most likely to be brought to Court, either because the parties feel they need an 'external force' or neutral arbiter to enforce a solution, or because they arouse the most bitter emotions, or because they feel it is feasible. In general it would seem that

---

[8] 'Family' is used in the European sense here, to denote disputes amongst the father's and mother's sides of families, or between husbands and wives, as well as disputes within matrilineal or patrilineal extended families. In the Akan areas of Ghana, matrilineal descent means that the wives/widows and children of a deceased man are not members of the *abusua* (blood family); hence the very common occurrence of disputes between a man's children and his matrilineal kin (siblings, nephews and nieces). But informants suggest that disputes within the blood family are also becoming more common, especially as the Intestate Succession Law, 1985 virtually created the conditions for litigation over the definition of 'family property', which depends upon showing a 'contribution' to the creation or purchase of the asset by any other family member.

family cases polarise the parties so bitterly that they are more likely to go to a state court.

Table 4.1: Breakdown of land cases by subject matter

|  | Valid % |
|---|---|
| Family dispute | 52.7 |
| Trespass/Boundary dispute | 17.7 |
| Unauthorised disposition of rights in land: by Chief/ Stranger | 12.8 |
| Other | 7.8 |
| Unauthorised sale of land | 4.9 |
| Dispute over cultivation/crops | 2.9 |
| Unauthorised disposition of land rights by Land Commission/ Government CPO | 1.2 |
| Total | 100.0 |

In fact, given what is known about the dynamics of large extended families such as are found in Ghana, it is not surprising that they are unable to resolve disputes over landed property amongst themselves in an amicable fashion. The bitterness once families fall out, especially over an inheritance, is such that an external and authoritative arbiter is essential. It could be that the lack of cases against government - in spite of the outcry about previous governments' record of improper land acquisition without compensation - simply reflects a reluctance to take on government, which can better afford an endless dispute than even the wealthiest private individual. This can only be speculation; what is clear is that the Courts are being overwhelmed with cases which reflect mainly the deep social conflict which is emerging from changes in the social and economic character of the Ghanaian family, particularly in our cases the matrilineal family. But the boom in litigation cannot be blamed entirely on the matrilineal system, given that in the Volta Region land cases dominate litigation in the courts even more than in Ashanti.[9] A more likely cause is the boom in urban development which is eating up the peri-urban areas of Accra, Kumasi and other main cities at a fantastic rate, much of it without planning permission or other legal title - a boom which is clearly proceeding without much legal challenge by the planning authorities.

---

[9] The Ewe people of the Volta Region have a patrilineal descent system.

The second issue relates to whether our litigants had gone to court only after exhausting all other possibilities - hence seeing Court as a 'last resort' when all else had failed - or whether they had deliberately made the state Court their first choice for resolving the dispute.[10] Again the survey produced a surprise finding: 47% of respondents had gone to a state Court first, without going through other kinds of dispute settlement procedure, showing that for the majority of the litigants, the Court was the preferred or most obviously appropriate way of getting their dispute resolved (although of course many of the defendants were dragged to Court by the decision of the plaintiffs). Overall, 37% of respondents had first tried to resolve their case using the chief, the elders or more formally, a 'traditional court' process. Only small numbers had used other kinds of dispute settlement, mainly family heads. There were significant differences between Kumasi and the other two locations here, in that in Goaso and Wa respondents were much more likely to have used a traditional court or the chief or elders first (Table 4.2), perhaps reflecting the more rural character of the catchment areas of those courts.

Table 4.2: Methods used to first settle a dispute, by location

| | Goaso Magistrate's Court | Kumasi High Court | Wa High Court | Total |
|---|---|---|---|---|
| State Court | 31.9% | 52.2% | | 46.1% |
| Traditional Court, Chief, Elders | 53.2% | 29.6% | 100.0% | 37.0% |
| Family | 8.5% | 8.1% | | 7.8% |
| District Assembly, Government Official | | 4.3% | | 3.3% |
| Between concerned parties | | 3.8% | | 2.9% |
| Police | | 1.6% | | 1.2% |
| CHRAJ | 2.1% | 0.5% | | 0.8% |
| Informal Arbitration | 4.3% | | | 0.8% |
| | 100.0% | 100.0% | 100.0% | 100.0% |

[10] This is an issue which is closely linked to debates about 'legal pluralism', with those who celebrate the coexistence of 'customary' and religious law administered by non-state dispute settlement institutions side by side with the laws of the state, arguing that 'forum shopping' benefits the poor and underprivileged.

The reasons which respondents gave for choosing the state Court, either immediately or after other methods had been tried , overwhelmingly reflected the perceived need for authority and certainty associated with court remedies. The largest group (33%) specifically mentioned the authority of the Court; others (28.3%) said they had become frustrated by the failure of the other party to respond or to come to an understanding and so a court action was seen as a way of using an authoritative force to get the issue resolved, whether the other party liked it or not. Many people commented specifically that arbitration was all very well but it lacked 'backing' and could not be enforced if the other party reneged on the agreement. There was also a suspicion about the impartiality of arbitration; one respondent said: 'Arbitration would not have helped because the one who would have sat on the case is part of the plaintiffs'. Many other comments were similar:

> "Whether Arbitration or Court what is needed is fairness. Arbitration has no backing."

> "Court is time wasting and high cost implication but I still prefer the court to Arbitration since as a stranger farmer, chiefs will be partial."

> "At the arbitration level she [the defendant] did not comply with the ruling thus I think at the court she will comply with the ruling so I prefer the court."

This craving for an authoritative settlement was even more marked in those who were asked to compare their earlier experiences of other forms of dispute settlement with the court: 73% said they wanted 'enforcement' of any judgment (assuming that they would win, of course), a perspective which probably reflects the dominance of 'declaration of title' as the most commonly sought remedy. Again there were some differences between Goaso and Kumasi on this issue, with Kumasi much more likely to cite the authority of the court as their main reason (39.2% as compared with 12%) and Goaso respondents more interested in forcing a resolution on the other party (39.4% as against 11.5%). But levels of education seemed to make little difference to the main reasons for going to court.

# 5. The Efficiency and Effectiveness of the Court System

## 5.1 Delays and adjournments

The survey confirmed what is already well known, which is that litigants, particularly in land cases, are experiencing severe delays. Of the respondents, 45% had filed their case more than two years previously, and another 25% had been coming to court for between one and two years (Table 5.1). Even more striking was the number of times people claimed they had had to attend court, mainly for the case to be adjourned without a hearing: 40.9% said they had attended court more than 21 times since the case began - a small group (6.1%) even claiming they had attended more than a 100 times. What is most significant about these findings however, is not so much the length of time cases have been going on, as the prevalence of 'adjournment'. The majority of the litigants whom we interviewed had experienced only preliminary hearings, or, more frequently, only adjournments after appearing before the judge. (Over the period of the survey we did not, of course, expect to find many cases which actually concluded with judgment given; only 9.5% of respondents had had a judgment). It could be said in fact that most of the frustration and inconvenience experienced by litigants is caused primarily by the adjournment practice, which constantly forces parties to attend court (and thus incur costs of time and money) to no apparent purpose. Why is adjournment such a major and indeed routine part of the experience of pursuing a case in court? If this could be understood, major improvements in the system could follow.

Table 5.1: Time since cases were first brought to court

|                    | Valid Percent |
| ------------------ | ------------- |
| Less than 3 months | 7.5           |
| 3-6 months         | 7.5           |
| 6 months to a year | 14.5          |
| 1-2 years          | 25.5          |
| 2-5 years          | 26.0          |
| Over 5 years       | 19.0          |
| Total              | 100.0         |

# ACCESS TO JUSTICE AND LAND DISPUTES IN GHANA
## Richard C. Crook

The litigants themselves, lawyers, judges, and court officials all have their own explanations or theories about the adjournment issue. Some litigants of course blame lawyers for simply not turning up when cases are scheduled, or for agreeing to postponements when asked to by the other party's lawyers or the judge. Lawyers certainly have to acknowledge this perception that they are not interested in concluding cases. But there is a surprising degree of agreement amongst litigants and lawyers that a major problem is parties themselves not turning up - principally defendants, but not exclusively so. In many cases plaintiffs themselves don't turn up for their own cases; one defendant we interviewed in Kumasi was enraged because for a whole year the plaintiff had never turned up, even though he had faithfully attended the court when the case was scheduled. It might be concluded that, in some instances, a court action is a form of harassment calculated to cause the defendant expense and inconvenience which can be prolonged by the necessity for continual adjournments. This is most obviously the case where plaintiffs abuse the court process by obtaining interim injunctions without any intention of seriously prosecuting the case. In many other cases, witnesses do not turn up. It is of course difficult to determine whether there is a 'chicken and egg' problem here; is failure to turn up caused by a well founded expectation that the case will be adjourned, or are adjournments caused by people not turning up? It could be that mundane conditions of Ghanaian life are to blame: transport difficulties, lack of cash, other more pressing engagements.

Whatever the reasons for the extensive degree of no-show on the part of litigants, lawyers agree that there are some administrative and legal/procedural problems to be tackled as well. Some cite a simple insufficiency of judges, caused by the unattractive pay and conditions; others say that there is too much reluctance to bring summonses for attendance and, in the event of that failing, moving for cases to be struck out for lack of prosecution. It is evident that many judges feel that lawyers themselves are often poorly prepared and fail to take appropriate actions on behalf of their clients, and fail to present clear or well documented cases. Judges themselves of course, could strike out cases if they are satisfied that the parties are abusing the process. In a recent 'backlog clearing' exercise the parties to 4,654 old cases were invited to appear before a Special Judge or face being struck out; the result was 77.5% reduction in the land cases on the books (Wood 2002). This outcome tells us little of course about the real reasons for the disappearance of these cases - it could be that they were effectively dead or ill-founded, the parties may have found other solutions, or, more worryingly, the de facto situation had simply been accepted, with whatever consequent injustice.

It is clear that there are some very simple administrative issues which could be tackled; the most obvious is the over-optimistic scheduling of hearings. If 20 or 30 cases are listed for a morning, the majority will be adjourned as a judge is likely to actually hear no more than three or four substantive trials in a session. It might be fairer to the parties if a realistic number of cases were scheduled for hearing and firm dates given, even if they are many months in advance. This would at least avoid the excessive number of wasted trips. Even simple things like making sure the parties know when the date and time of the next hearing is could be improved - in Goaso (where there are few lawyers involved) court officials help the litigants to remember when to turn up by giving them a slip of paper with the appointment written down.

Other administrative issues are less easy to tackle; lawyers and litigants also agree that many cases are adjourned because dockets 'go missing'. There is clearly a lack of capacity in the court administration; paper-based filing systems which are not up-to-date, manual typing and charges to clients even for typing of judgments. But are missing files caused by inefficiency and the lack of a decent filing system or is it caused by what some litigants (and lawyers) allege is deliberate mislaying of dockets by court staff, on behalf of the other party?

It is evident from the above that the issue of delay in the court systems is not simply a matter of 'too many cases'; the ways in which people use litigation, the administration of the courts, the behaviour of lawyers, court officials and litigants themselves, all play a part. And behind it all, is a special feature of the Ghanaian system: the almost total absence of out-of-court settlements. Judges and lawyers who were interviewed, and others who have written on this topic concur that when litigants file a land suit their prime motivation is to go to trial and get a court judgment. Very few are willing to entertain out of court settlements, although this is less so in commercial or contract cases. [11]The only explanation given is that land is somehow a more fundamental, non-negotiable issue; it is not substitutable, has symbolic value and of course increasing economic value both in the growing urban areas and as a security for retirement where there is no social security system. Attempts to encourage law firms to mediate between their clients, and proposals for a formal 'Court Masters' system for dealing with interlocutory matters seem to

---

[11] Kotey (2004) estimates that in only 8% of pending cases has there been any attempt at settlement, or 9% in the case of reported cases.

have come to nothing.[12] There are proposals for introducing ADR procedures backed by the court, but if this were to become compulsory, like Arbitrations in certain commercial matters, it could lead to undue pressure on weaker parties to settle.

*5.2. Costs*

Much is said about the cost of going to Court and the way in which it can exclude the poor in society from justice. But there are few reliable guides on how much it actually costs to take a land case through the court system, especially given the enormous variety in the length and complexity of cases and the number of times one has to attend court. It is certainly true that it costs more if a lawyer is used. In the High Court it is very difficult to do without a lawyer; in our two cases, 96.4% of respondents had employed a lawyer as compared with only 36.4% in the Goaso Magistrate's Court. We asked respondents if they could give an overall estimate of how much they had spent so far, and also asked them to break costs down by items if they could not give an overall figure. Just over half of them were able to give a figure (Table 5.2, next page). The modal amount was ¢2-5m, but only a small group (8.2%) had spent more than ¢20m.[13] Few were able (or willing?) to tell us how much they spent on their lawyers, but again the commonest amount given was 2-5 million, 70% falling within the ¢0.5-5m range.

¢20m is a lot of money for an average Ghanaian in regular employment, but the more common amounts (¢0.5-5m) are not as out of reach of a family or family segment acting corporately, or somebody with a farm or business, as might have been expected. The rural poor would of course be unlikely to have access to this kind of money.

---

[12] This observation is drawn from interviews with two leading Kumasi barristers and a Kumasi High Court judge in 2002-3.

[13] ¢20m, around GB£1200 at current rates, is the equivalent of four years' salary of a basic grade civil servant.

Table 5.2: Estimates of costs of bringing court action

| ¢ | Valid Percent |
|---|---|
| Nothing | 1.6 |
| Less than 100,000 | 4.9 |
| 100,000-500,000 | 7.4 |
| 500,000-2m | 21.3 |
| 2-5m | 31.1 |
| 5-20m | 25.4 |
| Over 20m | 8.2 |
| Total | 100.0 |

# 6 The Experience of Going to Court: How 'User Friendly'?

Perhaps one of the most critical issues in comparing land dispute settlement systems is to find a form of regulation which is simultaneously effective and yet also non-exclusionary, well understood and accepted as fair or legitimate. The only way to find out how litigants perceive the court system is ask them about their own experiences. But the court proceedings can also be observed in order to make a judgment on how the processes work in practice. We adopted both approaches.

The formal state courts inherited from the British colonial system have often been criticised by commentators both Ghanaian and foreign for being 'alien', intimidatory, and entirely unsuited to the norms of Ghanaian society. This rather exaggerated criticism often forgets that, although the core of the legal system - its concepts and rules - indeed remains the English common law, the courts have been operating in the country for well over a hundred years. During that time and especially after independence they have created through case-law and through judicial recognition of many rules of customary law, what could be now be called a 'Ghanaian common law'. And their procedures, as our evidence shows, have in many respects been 'Ghanaianised' too.

In physical appearance and the organisation of the hearing, it is true that the High Courts can seem intimidating. The public, witnesses and parties waiting to be called are physically separated by barriers and a deep well where the lawyers sit, nearest to the judge, whilst the judge is raised up high. Parties are called up to the bar inside the 'inner area' only when their evidence is required. It is often difficult to hear what is going on and judges and lawyers can often appear to be engaged in private conversations of a technical nature. Only a proactive and open judge can overcome these barriers by setting a good atmosphere in the court. The Goaso Magistrate's Court, by contrast, is an open-sided building located in a public area with no barriers between judge and litigants; whenever cases are being heard, members of the public are to be seen informally crowding around the court or sitting listening. It appears as a locally rooted institution (not least perhaps because of the public entertainment it provides).

Procedures in the Magistrate's Court are relatively flexible and informal, and lawyers only infrequently used. What is most interesting however about the procedures observed is that the British 'adversarial' format in which parties (and their lawyers) are supposed to each battle it out to demonstrate the truth of their cause, and the judge listens, has mutated into a much more 'inquisitorial' process more typical of civil law systems. The judge actively questions and cross examines the parties, seeking to clarify the stories and to establish the truth. The judge in Goaso did this in a highly interactive, informal and non-threatening way, allowing the parties to have their say. This is also happening in the High Court to some extent, primarily it would seem because lawyers are often so poorly briefed and incoherent that the judges frequently resort to speaking directly to the witness in an effort to find out what is being asserted and what points of law are relevant. Judges were also observed intervening in cross-examinations, helping witnesses to establish their points clearly, and indeed cross examining the lawyers themselves. If an interpreter is being used to translate into English, the judges often cut across an interpreter who is too slow or inaccurate and speak directly to the witness in the local language.

The issue of language is of course, even more critical than procedure or style. Again, the frequently heard assertion that the courts are incomprehensible to ordinary Ghanaians because they are based on English is quite wrong. English is only used where it is the common mutually understood language of the parties (particularly important in the multi-lingual northern areas of the country), otherwise a combination of English and the local language (Twi in Kumasi and Goaso) is the predominant mode, and the judge and the court clerks record the evidence in English. Overall, 63.2% of the respondents said that their proceedings were conducted in English and Twi, but this is somewhat misleading insofar as the different locations were very different in their practices: in Goaso, 70% of proceedings were in fact conducted all in Twi, whereas in Kumasi and Wa the predominant mode was a combination of English and one of the appropriate local languages (Table 6.1)

Table 6.1: Language used in court, by location

| | Goaso Magistrate's Court | Kumasi High Court | WA High Court | Total |
|---|---|---|---|---|
| Twi | 69.6% | 13.0% | | 25.9% |
| English | | 8.7% | 11.1% | 6.7% |
| English/Twi combination | 30.4% | 78.3% | | 63.2% |
| English/Waala combination | | | 66.7% | 3.1% |
| English/Sisala combination | | | 22.2% | 1.0% |
| | 100.0% | 100.0% | 100.0% | 100.0% |

To the evidence on language we can add the results of another more specific question in which we asked whether the respondents had understood what was going in the trial. Unfortunately as many had not experienced a full trial, many would not answer this question, although those who had felt they had heard enough on an adjournment hearing were willing to say something. Of those who answered, (61% of the respondents) 82% said they had understood the proceedings.

Given that judges in Ghana are adopting a more interventionist or inquisitorial style, the way in which they deal with the parties in front of them and indeed the whole atmosphere of the court as set by the judge determines in a very important way the perceptions which litigants have of the court process. Do they feel intimidated, do they think they have been fairly dealt with, had their point of view listened to? We tried to investigate this issue by asking litigants to describe how they felt the judge had spoken to them during whatever kind of hearing or hearings they had experienced. The results were quite robust and again challenge assumptions about the negative image which the courts are said to have.

Over half of all respondents described the judge in various combinations of positive terms, 'he speaks the truth' (a literal translation of the Twi phrase), he is 'patient', 'fair', 'helpful', and so on (Table 6.2, next page). A few said he was 'fast' - meaning conducted proceedings in a business-like manner, a comment which we allocated to the positive category. The most commonly used term, which emerged spontaneously in the pilot studies, was the 'truthful' comment. A few gave mixed answers, mostly to say that the judge had various good qualities but was too slow! (This was the predominant answer in Wa). As might be expected from the more informal atmosphere of the Goaso Magistrate's Court, the Goaso respondents were even more positive in their assessment than those in the Kumasi High Courts; but the difference comes largely from the fact that Kumasi litigants were more reluctant to give an opinion at all on the grounds that they had not experienced a trial.

Table 6.2: Perceptions of the judge's language and behaviour, by location

|  | Goaso Magistrate's Court | Kumasi High Court | Wa High Court | Total |
|---|---|---|---|---|
|  | % | % | % | % |
| Truthful, fair, etc. | 65.9 | 51.9 | 10.0 | 52.8 |
| Unhelpful, harsh, etc. | 2.3 | 1.9 | 10.0 | 2.3 |
| Slow | 0 | 2.5 | 0 | 1.9 |
| Mixed answer | 11.4 | 1.3 | 50.0 | 5.6 |
| Can't say - no trial | 9.1 | 35.0 | 30.0 | 29.4 |
| Can't say - not heard/ understood | 11.4 | 7.5 | 0 | 7.9 |
|  | 100 | 100 | 100 | 100 |

Moreover the Kumasi High Court litigants were overall more committed to the process than those in Goaso - 61.2% to 54.5%, reflecting the fact that Kumasi litigants were more likely to see the court as the first and most suitable place to take their case. Even more striking, the women litigants (most of whom were uneducated) were the most enthusiastic of all, 70.4% saying the case was worth it as compared with 53.7% of men, whereas the most highly educated were the most dissatisfied (only 40% said they thought it was worth it). We tested to see whether the 'worth it' answer was related to the kind of case being brought, but there were not major differences except that those who had cases involving unauthorised disposition by a chief or by a stranger were less satisfied (50%), suggesting that in these cases delay is critical. Once the land has been sold or disposed of to a third party it is very difficult to reclaim it, particularly after a long time interval. Finally as might be expected plaintiffs were more satisfied than defendants (64.9% as against 50.9%) no doubt because many of the defendants had been dragged to court very much against their will.[14]

Table 6.3: Overall, was it worth it to bring your case to court?

|  | Valid Percent |
|---|---|
| Worth it | 58.6 |
| Not worth it | 30.4 |
| Don't know | 8.0 |
| Mixed feelings | 3.0 |
| Total | 100.0 |

# 7. Conclusions

We began our research by asking some apparently simple questions: why do people go to the state court with their land cases? What is their experience of the court system, and are there any answers to the well-known problems of delay and expense which face those litigants? What we found suggests that it is not sufficient merely to blame Ghanaians for 'bringing too many cases', or to propose that there is an easy set of alternatives to the court system based on Alternative Dispute Resolution mechanisms. Our data certainly confirm the sobering dimensions of the crisis - the clear-up rate for pending land cases is not even keeping pace with the flow of new suits onto the books each year, so that total numbers are growing inexorably. Do the experiences of the litigants, lawyers and judges we spoke to provide any clues as to how to deal with this crisis?

*The need for authoritative remedies.* The most significant finding of the research is that, in spite of all the problems facing litigants when they enter the court system, there is a very strong demand for the authoritative remedies which a court backed by the authority of the state can provide. Once made, people's commitment to litigation is very strong. The extreme reluctance to entertain out-of-court

---

[14] The observations in this paragraph on the breakdown of responses to the 'was it worth it overall?' question are drawn from cross-tabulations of the Litigants' Survey full data set. Very few of our respondents had had a judgment entered (9.9%), but of those who had, 67% felt that the judgment was fair.

settlements is one indicator of this desire for a definitive remedy; another indicator is the extent to which the state courts are the first choice of large numbers of disputants—in some areas, the majority. Thus solutions based on the idea that a shift to ADRs - including renewed support for customary courts - will somehow relieve the pressure on the state courts are unlikely to be successful if they fail to provide an equivalent degree of authority and enforceability. One strand of reform could be to develop state-supported and -enforced ADRs (in effect a formalisation of out-of-court settlements) or other kinds of state supported tribunals, either at the local level or attached to the courts. But if parties cannot be persuaded to compromise and resolve their disputes by these methods, then they will still resort to the courts.

*The state courts still have the potential to offer popular and acceptable forms of justice.* The kind of adjudication experience offered by the courts is not as alien or inappropriate as many of its critics would have us believe. Although litigants are infuriated by the delays caused by constant adjournments, they generally respect the way the judges deal with them and most are not excluded by language or other factors from understanding what is going on. Litigants in our survey included a general cross section of the population both by sex and by class (although not by age), and even the least well educated had a generally positive view of the process, seeing it as an essential path to establish what they felt to be of deep importance to them. It is clear from the case analysis that family disputes are the main causes of litigation, rather than disputes between chiefs and their subjects or strangers/ indigenes, which are not appearing in court in the numbers which might have been predicted. In view of these findings, it would seem sensible to build on the more informal and flexible procedures which have developed in the Magistrates' Courts. The latter courts are key 'front-line' institutions operating at the local and rural levels, yet they are badly underesourced and short staffed. This is an allocation which it is perfectly possible to change within the context of a comprehensive programme of court reform.

*Reform of the court management and procedures is essential.* The above findings suggest that the courts themselves must be reformed and given more capacity to deal with at least some of this strong positive demand, rather than by-passed. Our analysis of cases and of the reasons for delay leads to the strong conclusion that a lot of improvement can be made by simple administrative reforms - the scheduling of cases for instance - and more use of legal remedies for striking out cases which are not being prosecuted properly.

*Overall there is a need for a combination of approaches and methods.* Given the numbers, neither the state courts nor ADRs can alone deal with the increasing pressure of land disputes. Thus on the one hand, new courts such as the proposed Land Division of the High Court have to be supplemented by invigorated Magistrates' Courts especially in the rural areas and possibly by District-level Local Advisory Committees on land matters as suggested in the National Land Policy. On the other hand, there is clearly a place for the promotion of ADRs where appropriate and acceptable, including court-supported ADR, and new forms of community-based ADR which are given state support in training and procedure. One state institution which is already providing a state-supported informal ADR service is the Commission for Human Rights and Administrative Justice (CHRAJ). But in the end , the state courts cannot be by-passed; they serve a very real popular need for authoritative justice.

# References

ALLOTT, Antony N.
1957    'Judicial ascertainment of customary law in British Africa.' *Modern Law Review* 20: 244-263. Reprinted at pp. 295-318 in Alison Dundes Renteln and Alan Dundes (eds.), *Folk Law: Essays in the Theory and Practice of Lex Non Scripta.* New York: Garland Publishing.
ANDERSON, Michael R.
2003    'Access to Justice and Legal Process: Making Legal Institutions Responsive to Poor People in LDCs.' *IDS Working Paper 178,* Law and Development Series. Brighton: Institute of Development Studies.
ATWOOD, D.A.
1990    'Land registration in Africa: the impact on agricultural production.' *World Development* 18: 659-671.
BASSETT, Thomas J. and Donald E. CRUMMEY (eds)
1993    *Land in African Agrarian Systems*, Madison: University of Wisconsin Press.
BENDA-BECKMANN, Franz von
2001    'Legal pluralism and social justice in economic and political development.' *IDS Bulletin* 32(1): 46-56.
BENDA-BECKMANN, Keebet von
1991    'Forum shopping and shopping forums: dispute settlement in a Minangkabau village, West Sumatra', *Journal of Legal Pluralism* 19: 117-

159.

BERRY, Sara

1993    *No Condition is Permanent. The Social Dynamics of Agrarian Change in Sub-Saharan Africa*, Madison: University of Wisconsin Press.

1997    'Tomatoes, land and hearsay: property and history in Asante in the time of structural adjustment.' *World Development* 25: 1225-41.

BRUCE, John W. *et al.*

1994    *Searching for Land Tenure Security in Africa*, Dubuque: Kendall.

CHANOCK, Martin

1991    'Paradigms, policies and property: a review of customary law of land tenure.' Pp. 61-84 in Kristin Mann and Richard Roberts (eds), *Law in Colonial Africa*. London: James Currey.

CHAUVEAU, J.P.

1997    'Jeu foncier, institutions d'accès à la ressource et usage de la ressource. Une étude de cas dans le centre-ouest ivoirien.' In: B. Contamin and H. Memel-Fotê (eds.), *Le modèle ivoirien en questions, crises, adjustements, recompositions*, Paris: Karthala/Orstom.

CROOK, Richard C.

1986    'Decolonisation, the colonial state and chieftaincy in the Gold Coast.' *African Affairs* 85: 75-105.

2001    'Cocoa booms, the legalisation of land relations and politics in Cote d'Ivoire and Ghana: explaining farmers' responses.' *IDS Bulletin* 32: 35-45.

DEBROY, B.

2000    *In the Dock. Absurdities of Indian Law*. New Delhi: Konark Publishers.

DEMBELE, O.

1997    'Le modèle d'urbanisme ivoirien face à la économique. Observations à propos de l'habitat métropolitain.' In B. Contamin and H. Memel-Fotê (eds), *Le modèle ivoirien en questions, crises, adjustements, recompositions..* Paris: Karthala/Orstom.

DFID (Department for International Development)

2000    *Safety, Security and Accessible Justice: Putting Policy into Practice*. London: DFID.

FARVACQUE, Catherine and Patrick MCAUSLAN

1992    *Reforming Urban Land Policies and Institutions in Developing Countries*, UNDP/World Bank/UNCHS Urban Management Program, Urban management Program No. 5. Washington, D.C.: World Bank.

FIRMIN-SELLERS, Kathryn and Patrick SELLERS

1999    'Expected failures and unexpected successes of land titling in Africa.'

*World Development* 27: 1115-1128.

FRED-MENSAH, B.K.

1999    'Capturing ambiguities: communal conflict management alternative in Ghana.' *World Development* 27: 951-65.

GHANA, REPUBLIC OF

1999    *The National Land Policy*, Accra: Ministry of Lands and Forestry.

2004    *Annual Report, 2004*. Accra: Judicial Service of Ghana.

GOCKING, Roger

2000    'The Tribunal system in Ghana's Fourth Republic: an experiment in judicial reintegration.' *African Affairs* 99: 47-71.

GRIFFITHS, John

1986    'What is legal pluralism?' *Journal of Legal Pluralism* 24: 1-50.

IIED (International Institute for Environment and Development)

1999    *Land Tenure and Resource Access in West Africa: Issues and Opportunities for the Next Twenty Five Years*. London: IIED.

KASANGA, R. Kasim *et al.*

1996    *Land markets and legal contradictions in the peri-urban areas of Accra Ghana: informant interviews and secondary data investigations*, Research Paper 127. Madison, Wisconsin: University of Wisconsin-Madison Land Tenure Center.

KASANGA, R. Kasim and Nii-Ashie KOTEY

2001    *Land Management in Ghana: Building on Tradition and Modernity*, London: IIED.

KEES VAN DONGE, J.K., 1999, 'Law and order as a development issue: land conflicts and the creation of social order in southern Malawi', *Journal of development studies* 36: 48-70.

KOTEY, Nii-Ashie

2004    'Ghana LAP Legislative and Judicial Review: Draft Report submitted to the Coordinator, Ghana LAP.' Accra: Ministry of Lands and Forestry.

LARBI, W.O., ANTWI, A. and OLOMOLAIYE, P.

2003    'Land valorisation processes and state intervention in land management in peri-urban Accra, Ghana.' *International Development Planning Review* 25: 355-371.

LÉONARD, É.

1997    'Crise économique, crise d'un modèle d'exploitation agricole. Ajustements et recomposition sociale sur les anciens fronts pionniers ivoioriens.' In B. Contamin and H. Memel-Fotê (eds), *Le modèle ivoirien en questions, crises, adjustements, recompositions*, Paris: Kathala/Orstom.

MAXWELL, D., LARBI, W.O., LAMPTEY, G.M., ZAKARIAH, S. and ARMAH-KLEMESU, M.

1999    'Farming in the shadow of the city: changes in land rights and livelihoods in peri-urban Accra.' *Third World Planning Review* 21: 373-91.

MCAUSLAN, Patrick

1998    'Making law work: restructuring land relations in Africa.' *Development and Change* 29: 525-552.

NADER, Laura

1979    'Disputing without the force of law.' *Yale Law Journal* 88: 998-1021.

2001    'The underside of conflict management - in Africa and elsewhere.' *IDS Bulletin* 32: 19-27.

PLATTEAU, Jean-Philippe

1996    'The evolutionary theory of land rights as applied to sub-Saharan Africa: a critical assessment.' *Development and Change* 27: 29-86.

RUF, F.

1985    *Politiques et encadrement agricole: partage des taches en Cote dIvoire*, Abidjan: IRAT/CIRAD.

SCHMID, Ulrike

2001    'Legal pluralism as a source of conflict in multi-ethnic societies: the case of Ghana.' *Journal of Legal Pluralism* 46: 1-47.

STREN, Richard

1989    'Urban local government in Africa.' In Richard Stren and Rodney R. White (eds), *African Cities in Crisis*, Boulder, Colorado: Westview Press.

VANDERLINDEN, Jacques

1989    'Return to legal pluralism: twenty years later.' *Journal of Legal Pluralism* 28: 149-157.

VAN LEEUWEN, F.K.C. and E.M. van STEEKELENBERG

1995    *The Process of Land Acquisition: A Case Study of Kumasi, Ghana.* Research Papers No 5. Amsterdam: Section Urban and Rural Planning in Africa. Ghana: Town and Country Planning Department, Ashanti Regional Office (Kumasi).

WOOD, G.

2002    'The courts and land dispute resolution in Ghana', paper delivered to the Land Disputes Settlement in Ghana seminar, Labadi Beach Hotel, Accra, 10-11 July 2002, Legal Pluralism and Gender Project, GTZ Ghana.

WOODMAN, Gordon R.

1996    *Customary Land Law in the Ghanaian Courts.* Accra: Ghana Universities Press.

2001    'Customary law in common law systems.' *IDS Bulletin* 32: 28-34.

# URBAN GOVERNANCE AND EMERGENT FORMS OF LEGAL PLURALISM IN MUMBAI[1]

Julia Eckert

## Legal Pluralism and the Selective State

Studies of legal pluralism in India have for long addressed the issue of the relation between state and non-state legal orders. Particularly the origin of the Indian state legal system in colonial rule has focussed discussions on the question of the imposition of a foreign normative system and its adoption and adaptation within Indian society. The supersession of traditional legal orders and the degree of their displacement by state law (Galanter 1997) have been at issue just as much as their resiliance and lasting determination of social order (Cohn 1959). At the same time that studies have examined the adaptation of state law to local practices others have shown the transformation of custom and religion through state codification (Kolff 1992), an issue that pertained particularly to the state's accommodation of legal pluralism through the personal status principle in family law.

Thus perspectives on legal pluralism have concentrated on the apparent dichotomy between customary legal norms (religious norms among them) and state law, and the negotiation of this dichotomy in the practices of the state as well as of its citizens. Because of this scholarly commitment to the 'entities' of custom and state law and their relationship, there has been little discussion of forms of legal pluralism that

---

[1] I am indebted to Franz and Keebet von Benda-Beckmann, Gerhard Anders and Werner Schiffauer for insightful comments and questions that helped me to improve and sharpen my argument.

emerge within the effective administration of justice and entitlements by state and non-state agencies.

It is banal to say that the administration of justice and of law and order in India is not concentrated in the state's hands (Baxi 1992, 100). Rather, it is fragmented and subject to situational constellations of actors that wield control and apportion rights. Various state and non-state agencies like different state agencies, community organisations, NGOs, and commercial (legal and illegal) enterprises, are involved in the governance of distribution, regulation and adjudication; these define legal institutions in their practices; they offer frames of interpretation and act themselves on specific interpretations of a legal framework; they set rules and practice sanctions and enforce thus certain norms and certain versions of a legal order.

These forms of legal pluralism shape much of everyday ordering and disputing in urban India. They relate to formal law and various customary legal orders equally in ways that are eclectic and pragmatic; they involve social norms filtered through the relations of power that shape them. They could be termed 'unnamed law' (F. v. Benda-Beckmann 1992, 2) as they do not refer to a specific basis of legitimacy, but rather are produced in the interactions within regimes of governance. These forms of legal pluralism are not new. They have for long determined the operative legal order of (urban) India (Chandarvarkar 1998), differing in the actors who had parts in their constitution, differing in the roles these different actors had within the constellations of governance, and differing as well in the power relations that determined these constellations. Their historic continuities and changes are not subjects of this paper; here these forms of legal pluralism are to be discussed in their relation to the emergence of what I want to call the selective state.

The selective state is determined by a particular division of labour, by particular processes of the formal and informal delegation and appropriation of governmental activities that differ from other such governmental divisions of labour, e.g. those constitutive of systems of indirect rule, or those envisioned by neo-liberal policies of public-private partnership - although they may result from such policies. The processes of the formal or informal devolution of judicial competences of the state to alternative organisations can take at least three principal forms: (a) The devolution of state productive and distributive tasks to private organisations like charitable organisations or commercial enterprises - that possibly also informally devolve regulation in as much as it is inherent in distribution and production. (b) The formal decentralisation and devolution of regulatory tasks in specific legal fields, be they of the kind of personal status regulations or the devolution of regulation for and jurisdiction over the internal affairs of corporations, but also of development projects and international NGOs. These will most probably also affect other legal fields than those specified, as well as persons not immediately part of the entity thus empowered. (c) The third process is the independent establishment of parallel centres of judicial authority that wield control over specific territories, specific groups of people or specific economic spheres and do not stand in a subsidiary, complementary relation to the state but in a parallel and autonomous one. The establishment of such autonomy has often been treated as a sign of state crisis, or the infringement of state sovereignty, of "fragmented sovereignties" (Randeria 2002). Such infringements have been associated with the autonomy of trans-national corporations and their regulatory autonomy but recently also with the 'project law' established by international development organisations (K. v. Benda-Beckmann 2001; Risse et al. 1999). Frequently, however, such autonomy and the associated ruptures of the integrity of the ideal-type modern state, and thus signs of its failure, have been seen in the establishment of local fiefdoms of criminal gangs, warlords, (neo-) traditional authorities etc. (Humphrey 1999; Schlichte and Wilke 2000; Volkov 2000).

In relation to the establishment of control by transnational corporations and also international (development) organisations, the active involvement of government in the fragmentation of state sovereignty has been demonstrated (Strange 1996; Likosky 2002; Randeria 2002). The appropriation of certain degrees of autonomy by sub-national entities within the selective state has been seen mostly as evidence for incomplete processes of state-building (particulary where such centres of authority refer to customary genealogies), or as signs of state crisis (Trotha 2000).

However, rather than such forms of legal pluralism being residues of incomplete state-building, or results of the incomplete expansion of the state legal and judicial system, it appears that such local, sub-national centres of governmental authority and their particular infringements of state monopolies, particularly those of coercive force and law, are also part of and embedded in functional regimes of governance that are shaped by the merger of processes of delegation and forceful appropriation, sometimes informal or unofficial.

On the one hand, this makes an idea of decentralisation and devolution that assumes the state to retain the competence to delegate competences obsolete; it becomes obvious that an operative legal order is shaped frequently by the interaction of various state and non-state agencies. The autonomy of the individual agencies within such constellations can differ; the state is not necessarily the one that regulates the relations among the others. On the other hand, the processes wherein devolution and appropriation merge show that the state is often deeply involved in the so-called 'informal', in the reproduction of informality and thus in the drawing of its own boundaries and limits. "The centrality of the state lies to a significant extent in the way the state organises its own decentering..." (Santos 1995: 118). However, selectivity of statecraft is not necessarily an integrated strategy, as the idea of the slim state would advocate. It evolves from possibly contradictory strategies of different state and non-state actors. It has its own dynamic, and its own rules that govern the cooperation and competition of these agencies.

The precarious interactions within these constellations of governance are evident in the new, or newly relevant forms of generation and administration of law in Mumbai (formerly known as Bombay.) The practices of one particular organisation active in the field of adjudication and law and order, namely the *Shiv Sena*, a regional political party of the Hindu Right, and its interaction with other organisations active in the field, show the merger of devolution and appropriation that characterise selective statecraft. On the one hand, the *Shiv Sena* is an extreme example to illustrate the emergence of new forms of legal pluralism: The *Shiv Sena* is an organisation whose domination extends from municipal and other regional public offices to a tightly nit network of local offices, its *Shakhas*, and thus spans the whole range of social and political life in the city. It is a political party, government (of the city of Mumbai), local NGO, social movement and (criminal) economic organisation all at once. Its degree of autonomy is high compared to NGOs, community organisations or even oppositional parties that are also involved in local governance. It is thus an extreme example for the issues in question because here the processes of the de-étatisation of regulation and adjudication involve a considerable degree of autonomous coercive force that has not been formally delegated by the state but has been appropriated by the *Shiv Sena* – although without much resistance from the state agencies, or maybe even with their connivance.

And thus the *Shiv Sena* is at the same time a mild example of the processes in question, not in terms of coercive force but in terms of its impact on state cohesion. The *Shiv Sena*'s autonomy and the legal order it has established are well integrated into the state order, treading the line, and shifting it, between norm breaking and norm setting. The organisation had been integrated thus even before it held public office, as its modes of operation have been instrumentalised for the strategies and agendas of various other agencies, namely those of industrial management, the Congress party for a period, for a later period the following national governing party, the BJP, and various other local interests.

The processes of delegation, devolution and appropriation are thus not always clearly distinct or distinguishable. Devolution to the *Shiv Sena* has often happened through neglect or default. Default has always had an ambivalent relation to intention. Instrumentalisation of the *Shiv Sena* by various other organisations was common and gave space to the activities of the party. But strategies of avoidance or simply lack of control were just as important in its establishment. Thus, differing and sometimes contradictory intentions combined and produced in the aggregation of their intended and unintended consequences spaces wherein the party could set its own rules. Thus it is also a clear example of the merging of informal devolution and forceful appropriation of normative control, and thus for the selectivity of state-craft. The *Shiv Sena*'s appropriation of normative authority, and its rupture of the state monopoly of coercive force, a monopoly which is usually seen as a distinctive characteristic of the state, does not imply a crisis of the state or its incomplete expansion.

I attempt here to sketch the processes that characterise the evolution of legal pluralism in the competitive relations of various institutions of governance by concentrating on one of these and on its position within this field. I want to discuss the establishment of the *Shiv Sena Shakhas* and their courts within the spaces opened by the promises as well as the inefficiencies and inaccessibilities of state services, that is, within the spaces created by the contradictions between the idea of the state and state practices. Their offers relate to tangible needs, but these needs are also defined by the aspirations of the developmental state. The normative order that they evolve in their practices is shaped by their political agenda but also remains bound to the normative offers of their competitors in the field of local order. The competition with these actors is shaped by rules that are generated by the integration and overlapping of various political and economic aspirations held by these different agencies, or by the networks involved in this competition. However, the competitive pressures that bind these various agencies to the interests of their clients and open up the operative legal order to change and adaptation are limited by the alliances, the cooperative relations and the divisions of labour that develop between some of the actors, and particularly those that involve state agencies. These divisions of labour are constitutive for the selective state, as they shape the processes of delegation and appropriation, the institutional specialisation and differentiation that dominate the operative legal order.

## The *Shiv Sena Shakhas*

The *Shiv Sena* was founded in 1966 by its still uncontested leader Bal Thackeray. First espousing regionalist claims within the newly created state of Maharashtra, it has made Hindu nationalism its central issue of mobilisation since the early 1980s. The party has been governing the city of Mumbai since 1985, and formed the state government of Maharashtra in coalition with the BJP (Bharatiya Janata Party) from 1995 to 1999. From 1998 until 2004 it was part of the governing coalition in the central government of India. Its distinguishing feature, however, is its strong local presence. It has established local party offices, the *Shakhas*, in every part of Mumbai as well as in most towns and villages of Maharashtra. These have become the dominant centres of local governance in many places, offering social services ranging from counselling and festivities to infra-structural improvements and protection.

The *Shiv Sena* and its *Shakhas* present themselves, and are seen by many people as providers who 'get things done'. The offer of efficient pragmatism answers to needs felt in many areas of the city. These needs are tangible but also shaped by the expectations and norms of governance that the promise of development by the state has affirmed. The state's ambiguous deliverance on its developmental promise - sometimes too much and often too little - opened spaces for the substitution for the state of various institutions, which constitute themselves bases of (local) power.

The *Shiv Sena* is explicit in its critique of the state and professes to correct both the 'excessive state', the inefficient, bloated, expensive, inaccessible bureaucracy as well as the 'insufficient state', the perceived failure of the state to fulfil its developmental promise. It thus connects to the widely asserted disillusionment over the capacity of state bureaucracies in matters of administrative services, and poses as a critic of both the bureaucratic organisation of the developmental state and the political deliberation in a parliamentary democracy. At the same time its leaders explicitly or tacitly answer to and reaffirm understandings of politics as the paternalist administration of distribution. They thus also cater to the idea of the providing and productive state once introduced by the Nehruvian ethos, and turned into mass populism by Indira Gandhi's programme of *Gharibi Hatao* ('abolish poverty'). Bal Thackeray calls for 'benevolent dictatorship', and lays the blame for state inefficiency on parliamentary procedures and on democracy which in the *Sena*'s view are responsible for corruption and indecision. "What is politics? Politics is just good administration. So our politicians don't know politics," was the opinion of the *Shiv Sena* leader Shrikant Samolkar. "They just come and talk and go. We solve their problems," felt Vinodh Kumble, an older member of the movement. Many party members of the *Shiv Sena*, the *Sainiks* (soldiers), claim that their own activities are not 'politics', but are instead based on 'obvious' notions of what is good and what needs to be done. *Sainiks* have projected their acts of protest and their acts of resolution as a model for a counter-project of politics. Thus 'getting things done' is their credo. Direct action replaces parliamentary politics and is superior in efficiency and moral rectitude.

The party's *Shakhas* are thus a 'better state', a 'benevolent dictatorship' on a local scale; they profess to fulfil what the state promised but failed to deliver. They supplement various functions that in India are usually associated with the state. They offer local services; they organise infrastructural measures such as water connections, garbage collection, public toilets or roads; they initiate employment schemes, youth activities, crèches and tutoring; they put up festivals, help in obtaining admission to schools; and thus address a wide variety of concerns and every-day issues of urban life.

Along with these distributive and productive tasks come regulatory functions inherent in the organisation of allocation. The *Shiv Sena* explicitly takes on regulatory functions, as the party connects its local formal and informal governance role to its particular concepts of substantive rights. True to its stance of defending the claims to the city of those who 'were there before' against those who have come later, enemy images have been the mainstay of the *Sena*'s postures. It has always attributed the ills it detected in society to specific social groups and thus personalised the civic crisis of the city. The party does not call for structural changes, revolution or reform; rather, it calls for the elimination, in whatever way, of those it holds guilty for the identified malaise. The targets are interchangeable: it is its mode of distinguishing between friend and foe rather than specific public enemies which characterises the *Sena*'s ideology. What is common to the depictions of all of its enemy images is that they are made out to be existential threats to the lives and livelihoods of every 'good Indian'. The justification for the urgency to fight them lies in their portrayal as being connected with larger threats, be they Pakistan, Islam or the Soviet Union or the general category of 'evil' in the form of decadence, dishonesty, poverty, crime, dirt, scarcity. And it is the alleged hold on the Indian state of these 'enemies' which is the real threat to legitimate citizens of that state.

The identity of these threatening 'others' has often been related to the *Sena*'s electoral strategies. Especially since its expansion into the BMC they are frequently those who "... won't be able to cause us damage since they haven't been included in the voting list," as Manohar Joshi explained when he was still Chief Minister.[2] Thus at the same time that the party pours forth exclusionary vituperations, it engages in a populism of many forms which suggests integrating almost anybody into the category of the

[2] Manohar Joshi in an interview in the *Indian Express*, 17.1.1998.

'legitimate ingroup'. Thus the culprits of scarcity and threat to one's status are always 'the others'. In all cases the *Sena* retains the claim to define the legitimate in-group and affirms this claim with violence. It is a fundamental delineation of legitimate and illegitimate citizens.

These possessive claims of the party are also expressed in the many renamings of the city's public buildings, streets and, of course, of the city itself, with names that suggest the conquest of the city for its allegedly original proprietors, the *Marathi Manoos*. However, rather than those claims the regulation implicit in the *Shakha's* distributive and productive tasks shapes the operative rules of many of Mumbai's neighbourhoods. As centres of distribution the *Shakhas* are accessible and therefore relevant to the organisation of everyday life. They become the vehicle of regulation in many matters, implicitly in their underlying ideas of just allocation, but most clearly in their administration of local disputes.

## Adjudication in the *Shakha*

The *Shiv Sena* has established an informal system of 'courts' within its *Shakhas*. These courts deal with disputes relating to everyday living in the city, with quarrels over water taps and other public property, neighbourly tensions, family matters, conflicts over property, contracts and debts, questions of land ownership and alimentation, labour issues, harassment and violence. Issues range from disputes about the rights to a specific location for a hawker's stall, quarrels about garbage dumps or noise, issues of petty crime and cheating, to litigation over loans and property and real-estate disputes, which easily become deadly serious in a real-estate market like Mumbai's. Thus they deal with civil as well as criminal matters, and often also with administrative regulation.

Mostly issues are brought before the *Shakhas Pramukh*, the leader of a *Shakha*, by one of the litigants; sometimes the *Shiv Sena* intervenes on its own initiative.[3] Court

---

[3] In all cases observed there was a class imbalance as the members of the *Shakha* all came from more secure economic backgrounds than their clients. This also meant that there was a deference relating not only to the status arising from the court room interaction but also a more general status difference. The latter involved considerable degrees of deference on the part of the clients. These were difficult to distinguish from the awe or fear inspired by the party's reputation for 'effective delivery'. The party also engages in dispute resolution among clients who hail from wealthier

sessions are short; most disputes are resolved in one sitting. Judgments are swift and produce clear-cut decisions. They attempt to produce the results demanded by the party whose claims are upheld: a piece of land changes ownership, a building is demolished, a garbage dump is removed, a hawker is expelled, money is paid, or not, a divorce takes place, etc.

Judgments are certain to be carried out - and that is one reason for the use of the courts - as they are swiftly enforced by the *Sainiks* of the *Shakha*. Thus women *Sainiks* prided themselves on their efficacy: "When we ask a man to come it is an order." "We threaten them to ensure that they do whatever we say." "If they do not come they will regret it." "They know we'll use violence," insisted young women *Sainiks* on the occasion of the former leader of the *Mahila Aghadi*, the *Shiv Sena*'s women's wing, Sudha Churi, holding her weekly court at *Shiv Sena* Bhavan.

*Shakha* Pramukhs insist that their rulings are guided by common sense. Quite a few of the Pramukhs have legal training. But they insist the *Shakhas* - like *Lok Adalat* courts of the state judicial system - are not the place for legal intricacies that 'the common man is tired of' but for common sense and effective and conclusive agreements. 'Common sense' implies that the status of the litigants as well as their position within social relations are taken into account in various ways, since the rights of individual litigants, and thus the solution to a dispute, are inherently connected to their role and position within the local context. However, *Shakha* rulings do not necessarily aim at recreating a status quo and repairing the social relations possibly impaired by a dispute. Rather, they take into account what they assume to be considered each litigant's rightful due, but they also have to consider their relations to his other activities and concerns in a locality. The *Shakha Pramukh*'s rulings are part of the social capital he accumulates; he has to balance 'popular opinion' against his social networks.

Thus the notion of 'common sense' involves implicitly the *Shiv Sena*'s notions of the proper order, but is intricately linked to local social relations.

segments of society. These disputes are, however, seldom dealt with at the *Shakhas*' court sessions but rather in the offices or private residences of the *Shakha Pramukhs*.

## Modes of Legitimation

The establishment as well as the use of the *Shiv Sena* courts by the clients of the party arises from the inefficiency and inaccessibility of the state courts. These are due to the immense backlog in state courts resulting from procedural problems of the Indian legal system. This is reflected both in the explanations of people who have sought the assistance of the *Shiv Sena* courts as well as in the self-representation of the *Shiv Sena*.

> For the people, anything is better than paying lawyers' fees and then waiting endlessly for judgments. We have had *lok panchayats* [local governing councils] long before they were introduced by law and I think this is just like common *lok adalat* [customary law], as now favoured by the government.[4]

The party's justifications of its courts thus often speak the same language as and are in line with widely advanced analyses of the crisis of the state judicial system (for example World Bank 2000). They are part of the party's general claim that its *Shakhas* fulfil state tasks better than the state itself.

The *Shiv Sena*'s criticism of, and distinction of its own institutions from state agencies is not expressed in terms of the norms and values of state law but in terms of the alleged inefficiency and inaccessibility of state procedures. The significant exception to this is the party's advocacy of the introduction of a uniform civil code, that is in line with the stances of its ideologically more radical Hindu-nationalist allies of the Sangh Parivar, as well as the party's militant opposition to caste based quotas[5] and minority rights, But the *Sena*'s courts do not contest the validity of state law. They do not name an alternative normative order as more valid or legitimate, and do not, for example, refer to religious law or other sources of legitimate ideas of justice. Rather, the *Shakhas* contest the efficiency and accessibility of state courts.

Thus, the norms that are explicitly and most regularly espoused are pragmatism, common sense and efficacy. The *Sena*'s courts are presented as accessible and therefore as more participatory and 'close to the people'. They are presented as

---

[4] Sudha Churi, former leader of the *Shiv Sena*'s women's wing *Mahila Aghadi*, during an interview in March 1997.

[5] The party has for many years favoured (and fought for) regional quotas and son-of-soil policies, while always denouncing caste-based quotas as divisive.

representing the 'common man's' sense of justice and as making that sort of justice available to that very 'common man'.

Thus, in the courts as well as in its administrative role in the localities of Mumbai the *Sena* claims to be 'the better state'. This is one aspect of their reference to institutions such as *Lok Adalat*,[6] that have recently been revived by the State Legal Aid Authority to solve the problem of backlog of cases. This promotes the idea that the *Shakhas* are deeply embedded in local or 'traditional' culture and therefore 'close to the peoples' minds', but also the idea that they are already practising what modern statecraft is only now discovering to be beneficial models of conflict resolution. They thus allegedly respond simultaneously to the value systems of Indian tradition and the modern state. They seem to affirm the status of both, the institutions as well as the traditions used to justify them, pointing towards both the primaeval age of these traditions and their concurrent modernity.

The criticism of legal procedures as inefficient, and the concentration on substantive law is central to the transformations of material law effected by the appropriation of regulative tasks by the *Shiv Sena*. The substantive content of the legal institutions that the *Shiv Sena* refer to is defined by the party's practices. Thus, *lok adalat* is what the *Shiv Sena* does in its courts anyway; *mediation* "like you in the West also have now"[7] is what the *Shakha Pramukh* has long done when presiding over the courts; *human rights*, and *'the right to self-defence'*[8] is what is declared by the *Shiv Sena* to be 'nationalist and human'[9] and justification for the party's anti-Muslim stance.

Thus, its overall Hindu-nationalist stance becomes central to the interpretation of justice. In the *Shiv Sena*'s courts the party's opposition to personal law, to caste-based reservations or to minority rights are less significant as these are legal issues that the

---

[6] *Lok adalat* was once introduced as a local form of judiciary connected to the *panchayat* system, the village councils, to administer state law by the state itself as part of its decentralisation programme (Galanter 1997: 68). Nowadays *lok adalat* courts are part of the judicial reform programme introduced by the central state to function as institutions of mediation (Galanter and Krishnan 2002; Whitson 1992).

[7] *Shiv Sena* leader Madhokar Sarpotdar in an interview, February 1997.

[8] "The right to self-defence is bestowed upon every citizen by the constitution." Saamna 9.1.1993

[9] Saamna, 29.4.1998

*Shakhas'* courts rarely deal with. More significant are the party's ideas of who are legitimate participants in entitlements and rights, and its vision of the nation and of the proper order that underlie its rulings. It draws a militant line between those who rightfully belong and those who are deemed outsiders and who are thus illegitimate participants.[10] It holds an idea of order that basically stresses the harmonious body politic, denouncing claims to equality or merely equal rights as 'selfish' and potentially dangerous self-interests that destroy the unity of the community. Although the party sometimes espouses class rhetoric ("I believe that only two castes exist in this world: the poor and the rich. There is no third caste,"[11]), paying heed to the large working class segment among its supporters, it vigorously propounds the necessity of this communal unity in the face of alleged threats by the identified 'enemies' of Hindu culture.

## Pluralist Pressures

The processes described above could be analysed as the shift from the rule of law to the rule of force. However, this rule of force is precarious. The normative order that is established through the effective administration of justice by the *Shiv Sena* is not

---

[10] Within the logic of competitive patronage the exclusionary principles of the *Shiv Sena* are partly modified. Populism takes precedence. As long as people seek access to the *Shiv Sena*, they can avoid the possible stigma of being illegitimate participants in the city's largesse - at least as long as their votes are considered relevant. Belonging to the *Sena* is a means of belonging to the legitimate in-group simply because the Sena relies on its mass base. As a political party with aspirations to acquire formal positions in government, and therefore tied to democratic procedures, it is interested in as large a mass-base as possible, no matter how it is gathered. Where minority groups or those that the party defines as the public enemy are relevant in terms of local elections, their demands may, at least temporarily, be considered. A continuous example of this opportunism is the party's stance towards the rights and demands of the various *Dalit* groups in the city and the state of Maharashtra. Generally fiercely opposed to politically organised *Dalits*, and often having made explicit this opposition with violence against *Dalit* organisations, the *Shiv Sena* has wooed all sections of the *Dalits* ever since they entered into a successful coalition with the Congress party and the National Congress Party (NCP) and ousted the *Sena* from the state government in 1999.

[11] Thackeray in an interview with *Onlooker*, May 16-31, 1981.

hegemonic. The operative legal order is plural in the sense that it is precarious, that it is constantly open to adaptations and changes that result from plural pressures and the competitive normative offers of various actors in the field of adjudication, be they other private or community organisations or the state. The operative legal order thus sways between phases of monopolisation and dominance and phases of pluralisation and adaptation.

*Shakha Pramukh*s are not the only providers of services, and they compete with a variety of 'local leaders', social workers - a rather vague term which can refer to a wide array of activities in the city -, *dadas* (strongmen), 'slumlords', *goondas* (local gangsters), as well as self-help organisations, NGOs and the police in the field of setting rules and generating law (see also Panwalkar 1998). The institutions of *Dada* and *Dalal* (middle men) have been part of the city's modes of governance ever since its rapid expansion during industrialisation (Chandavarkar 1981; 1994: 168-238). The *Shiv Sena* has in no way driven out other organisations, nor has it won predominance over its competitors everywhere. The degree of dominance of the *Shakha* differs from area to area and depends on various factors: the strength of the competitors, be they gangs or *dadas*, political parties or NGOs; it depends on the potential of the area in terms of revenue and votes; or the need in an area for extra-state services. In some areas the *Shiv Sena* is hardly active at all, for example in some of the Muslim areas of central Mumbai, but also in others where it has lost the competition with its rivals or where the specific services of the organisation are of little value to the residents.

The positions of the various agents in matters of conflict, distribution and allocation have always been precarious (Chandavarkar 1998: 191-193). They have been and are restricted by demands of reciprocity, competition with rivals, and the expectations of their clients. Communities can and do reject leaders (Panwalkar 1998). Moreover, the term 'community leader' is often misleading. It assumes a higher degree of social integration of neighbourhoods than is often the case. It assumes a higher degree of authority than those leaders necessarily hold: their 'lead' is often situational, as is the 'community', which is formed around particular issues. As a 'community' they make use of 'community leaders' in particular situations when such collective representation is demanded in dealing with an outside situation, whether it concerns the state or another 'community'. Thus, leaders are leaders in particular situations and the integration of the entity they represent is often subject to the issues at hand.

Thus, the sway of self-proclaimed leaders is shaky. The influence of the *Dalals* derives from their connection to political parties. Political parties are interested mainly in voters. Local leaders, in order to be able to provide parties with voters and thus get influence within the state administration, which is the base for their local support, need to pay heed to the interests of the residents - as these have the option of favouring the competitor. The competition between various local leaders or local strongmen over an area constitutes a possibility for the residents of an area to bind these local leaders to their interests. Thus, because of the direct or indirect involvement of these various local agencies in democratically organised party politics, competition means the adaptation to demands from the side of voters as well as to the offers to voters by competitors.

This also holds for the competition of *Shakha Pramukhs* over party posts within the party structures. For party-internal competition the rule is: "If you can't bring a mob you are a flop," as one *Shakha Pramukh* who hoped to rise high in the party put it in an interview. A 'mob' can be bought, but a 'mob' knows its price. And a 'mob' is a 'mob' only when the right price is paid. Otherwise it is a 'community' with its own priorities and demands on the bidders. One housing society within Dharavi, allegedly Asia's biggest slum, agreed to operate as a 'mob' in turn for the improvement of local water connections. Earlier the society 'had been Congress'. But after the Congress candidate failed to deliver, the society, under the leadership of a few of its residents, turned against their president and took up the repeated offers of the *Shiv Sena* corporator, then collectively - but not necessarily unanimously - voting for the party. Another housing society in another area of the city demanded public toilets in return for agitating publically for a *Shiv Sena* leader. They were indeed awarded with toilets, and had previously had their paths paved by the *Shiv Sena* corporator.

Whether the exchange of patrons is possible and is actually done is dependent on whether the competitors of the *Shiv Sena* in the area are alternative political parties or commercial criminal enterprises. In the latter case many will prefer the *Shiv Sena*'s demands for donations to that of a purely criminal gang, as the gangs are less efficient in bringing about public services, being less well connected to the Municipality than the *Shiv Sena*. As one resident of Sion, an area in Mumbai, laconically stated:

> Costs have not gone down. What we now give as donation we gave
> as protection money before. They say it's for cleaning up the area.
> And they say that they cannot guarantee security otherwise. We all
> know what that means! But we still prefer them [the *Shiv Sena*]. At
> least you know who you are talking to.

If however the *Shiv Sena*'s competitors are other political parties with an alternative system of patronage or their own party comrades, the competition will take a different course.

The influence of the competing bidders is thus dependent on the offers they can make in terms of civic priorities and the demands of areas, even where the competition between the various agents has turned into an arms race, as at times it has.

However, while the *Shiv Sena* competes in terms of clients with NGOs, community leaders or *dadas*, and while it competes for these clients in terms of votes with other political parties, it has an advantage in its integration of the various formal and informal positions of power. This advantage is shared with few other organisations, and when the party perceives competition as threatening its specific offer and thus its niche in the landscape of relations of domination, its reaction is fierce. It once virtually eliminated the gang of underworld don Arun Gowli with the help of the police. Gowli had started *Shakhas* himself and had been successful in attracting many *Sainiks*.

Thus the checks and balances inherent in the competition and the dependency on voter support are precarious as the *Shiv Sena* can, where it has enough strength, eliminate its rivals. More importantly, some of its competitors, particularly the Congress party, have made good use of the *Shiv Sena*'s services themselves and have locally developed more cooperative than competitive relations with the *Shiv Sena* (Gupta 1982, 176-177; Ribeiro 1998). Alliances between various political competitors restructure and diminish the checks and balances inherent in their competition over voter support. At the same time, party alliances do not diminish internal party competition. Thus, as already stated, the rule that 'If you can't bring a mob you are a flop' binds *Pramukh*s with aspirations to higher party posts to the frequently diverse interests of their local clients.

In Mumbai it is the rules of the common political space which most of these actors are directly or indirectly involved in. These are the rules of mass politics: 'If you can't bring a mob you are a flop.' In Mumbai, the power of the various actors and the establishment of monopolies over jurisdiction and legislation are always subject to the competition within the democratically organised access to control. The rules which govern the chances to succeed in this competition are those of democratic party competition - because those offices that are acquired through democratic means are also those which provide the easiest access to and control over the still lucrative resources of the state. In many ways the terms of the competition between the various agencies active in the field of adjudication and regulation, up to the competition between *Shakha Pramukh*s over party posts, are thus structured by state law.

## Strategic Adaptations

Thus, even where the *Shiv Sena* has established an institutional dominance within the local constellation of governance, the rules that shape the operative legal order are subject to adaptation. The *Shiv Sena* is particularly adept at adapting its methods to local moods as it has never shown much concern for programmatic consistency but has favoured action. "I don't believe in programmes," declares Bal Thackeray. "In the last 40 years too many manifestos have been published and then consigned to the dustbin. I believe in implementing..." The party has shown a considerable degree of flexibility, or perhaps opportunism. Once, for a period of two weeks, it even voiced socialist demands. Its vague reference to all sorts of traditions and its practice of singular rulings specific to a case keeps its 'content' flexible, to be adapted to opportunity structures in the public discourse. It can shift its militancy from one daily issue to the next and re-interpret its agenda in terms of the demands made by its clients and in terms of public discourses. Thus the 'occupation' of a definition of a legal institution is never complete, nor is the definition of the *Shiv Sena* itself final, but always dependent on the relations determining the specific issue at hand.

One example of strategic adaptations to changing demands by clients would be the definition of women's rights as practised in the *Shiv Sena* courts, as they often deal with family matters of alimentation and violence. Women's rights are generally one of the favourite subjects of Hindu-nationalist organisations that have been skilful in using the "obvious popularity of women's issues" (Setalvad 1995, 240; see also Agnes 1995). Within their agenda, women's rights are redefined in terms of communal antagonism: Protecting women's rights turns into a way of protecting Hindu culture (and protecting Muslim women from their men). Thus, the issue of women's rights is transformed from one of gender relations into one of a struggle between two communities. 'The Muslim' is constructed as the violator of women: the violated 'his own' women - the possessive language recurs in this discourse - by Islamic family law, polygamy and triple talaq. He violates Hindu women by their rape and abduction throughout history and especially at the time of partition (where the same acts by Hindu or Sikh men are termed simply retaliatory). And thirdly, he violates the country, *Bharat Mata*, Mother India by 'her' partition (Butalia 1995, 69), for which

Muslims are held responsible. Women's honour, thus, is conflated with the protection of India and 'Indian tradition' and the practices which go along with it.[12]

In the daily practice of the *Shiv Sena* these issues are often dealt with in contradictory ways, differing from one *Shakha* to the other, as well as depending on the specific local constellation and demands. A 'feminist' tune is often voiced particularly by women *Sainiks* to legitimise many of the *Mahila Aghadi*'s activities. Their justification of their role as arbiters in marital disputes was regularly couched in terms if a pro-woman attitude.[13] The women *Sainiks* usually claimed that they took up the women's cause in the marital disputes brought before them and proudly related how they forced men to comply with their commands by threatening them and publicly humiliating them.

However, some *Pramukh*s described how they had also told the women of 'their duties as wives.' In one case, a husband was granted permission to obtain a 'customary divorce' because he and his family felt that the young wife did not work hard enough in the home. He claimed that the failure of the marriage was entirely his wife's fault, and therefore he demanded to retain the dowry payments. The *Shakha Pramukh* granted the husband a divorce and the dowry. The family of the women unhappily agreed to a divorce largely because her in-laws had started to physically

---

[12] The disputes and contradictions in the debate about women's rights within the Hindu nationalist movement, for example on the issue of *Sati* among prominent women of the *Sangh Parivar*, do not exist within the *Shiv Sena*. Unlike the *Sangh Parivar*'s women's organisation, but like the BJP's *Mahila Morcha* or the VHP's *Durga Vahini, Shiv Sena* displays no public discord. This is possibly because the *Mahila Aghadi* is, like the *Shiv Sena* in general, little concerned with ideological intricacies or contradictory interpretations of Hindutva and women's role in it. Not only is the line given by Bal Thackeray decisive, but its vagueness integrates contradictions. Moreover, the *Mahila Aghadi*, too, believes in 'getting things done' rather than thinking about the nature of *Shivshahi*. Disputes here concern rather the control of and rights to certain territories and their revenue, posts and responsibilities.

[13] The fact that in all the cases described the man had been found 'guilty' and had been punished may be due to the fact that it was assumed that such a 'feminist' logic would find legitimacy with the western listener. It is noticeable how much stress is put on the defence of women's rights and feminist rhetoric, and relatively little on the nationalist and communalist foundations of the women's agenda of the *Mahila Aghadi*.

abuse the wife, and her mother wanted to save her lest she should be seriously harmed. But they wanted to retrieve the dowry and also did not want the name of their daughter further sullied by the allegations of her in-laws that the failure of marriage was due to her being an unfit wife, since this would have made the prospects for a second marriage even more remote. A local NGO stepped in and managed to retrieve the dowry for the young woman by proving that the young man had indeed made use of his wife's wifely duties and had at the same time started an affair with another woman, thus indicating his failures in the marriage. The *Shakha Pramukh* reversed his ruling accordingly. This was a result of the NGO mobilising the neighbourhood to speak up about their knowledge, mobilising public opinion so to say, but also of their threatening the husband with a divorce in court which he feared would take far too long for his desires.

In their 'common sense' judgments in family disputes the *Mahila Aghadi* uses a model of order which lies firmly within the patriarchal fold, where women and men have duties and rights according to their roles in the patriarchal family. However, they adhere to the normative standards of other agencies when they are compelled to do so by 'public opinion'. Moreover, state courts and the state legal system often remain the frame of reference. On the one hand they pose a threat, above all because of the immense amount of litigants' time they consume. But on the other hand they extend a promise within a normative system of specific rights that people can claim in their disputes even outside of these state courts, for example through local NGOs that employ them together with the threat of formal litigation. Thus, adaptive changes are situational and local and depend on the terms of alternative normative offers in the context. While in one case a *Shakha Pramukh* might grant permission for a divorce to a husband not satisfied by the services of his wife, or tell a women demanding alimentation from a gambling or drinking husband of her wifely duty to endure and send her away, in another case a *Pramukh* might gather a group of *Sainiks* (women or men), search for the husband, beat him up and threaten him with further action if he does not comply with his duties as head of the family.[14]

More complex are the programmatic adaptations of the *Shiv Sena* regarding labour issues. Here, the *Shiv Sena* has also espoused contradictory positions, not only

---

[14] Thus happened to a couple where the wife had complained to the local *Shakha* that her husband was spending the little money he earned on drinking and on other women. The wife was ambivalent about the result of her action as her husband was unable to work for several days after the judgment had been imposed and thus she had to rely again entirely on her own meagre earnings and look after her husband as well.

consecutively but even simultaneously. It generally favours a management-friendly policy and self-help schemes for those made redundant (Purandare 1999: 91). In particular the failure of the textile strike in 1982 and the progressive de-industrialisation of Mumbai serve to support the argument of many *Sainiks* that only through cooperation between management and workers can both profit. Many *Shiv Sainiks* - but certainly not all - are convinced that strikes are as bad for the workers as for the management and above all for the nation. "We don't subscribe to the notion that the owner is an enemy. Large hearted and good owners are not our enemies, and we will never organise strikes in factories whose owners identify themselves with the interests of the workers and the interests of Maharashtra," proclaimed Bal Thackeray (Purandare 1999: 91). "The workers will be taught to produce more and only then ask for more," says the guidelines for the BKS published in *Marmik*, the *Shiv Sena* weekly magazine in 1968.

The *Shiv Sena* has affirmed this stance by busting unions unfavourable to management (Gupta 1982; Purandare 1999). It has often been able to gain employment for its own clients when members of radical unions were sacked. According to oppositional unionists, the management of many a company encouraged the establishment of *Shiv Sena* unions in its factories when, for example, the militancy of factory-based unions made it seem beneficial to have an internal union with a 'cooperative' outlook. Many a time *Shiv Sena* leaders have placed their clients in the jobs of workers who had been sacked in the course of labour agitation. This was a strategy largely confined to unskilled jobs. In the process non- *Shiv Sena* unions lost their support base because their support base lost their jobs.

In the long run, this trapped the *Shiv Sena* unions in a difficult position because they had to pay heed to the demands of the new workers, who were the party's clients. Thus, occasionally the party has taken up labour issues in a manner that opposed management strategies. On April 25th 2001, for example, the *Shiv Sena* Unions took part in a general *bandh* (closure, strike) protesting against the government's suggestions to make labour laws more flexible (Hensman 2001). This measure was clearly out of line with their general management-friendly stance and their hostility to militant unions. Earlier they had taken up the workers' opposition to the closure of the Balco steel plant in Chhattisgarh. Both were possibly strategies to strengthen the *Sena*'s base among unionised workers.

In the *Shakha* courts, *Pramukh*s deal mostly with the so-called informal sector, i.e. with employers and employees of enterprises that employ officially less than 100 workers and which are in consequence not subject to many of the labour regulations.

Injury, unpaid wages or delays in payment, as well as petty theft or shirking are the most common issues. Redundancies and compensation are not dealt with here as employment in these industries is mostly highly irregular. *Pramukh*s assert that their rulings in labour disputes are guided by pragmatic reason and 'common sense'. It was common sense, for example, that children of poor people could be employed - contravening child labour laws - because poverty makes this necessary and 'these children would otherwise go hungry'. Common sense also implied that they do not enjoy the same rights as adult employees - thus contravening labour regulations - but that they cannot be expected to work as hard and as long as adults. In one case, a boy had been badly injured, losing his right hand. The employer cancelled the employment. The boy was the sole bread winner in a family consisting of his aged grandmother and a mentally disturbed mother. A local NGO demanded the employer pay compensation. The *Shakha Pramukh* ruled that the employer did not have to pay. After the NGO mobilised the neighbourhood, the employer offered to take the boy back at a lower wage. The *Shakha Pramukh* told people not to address the NGO with their matters. The NGO again mobilised public opinion and threatened court action. It succeeded in making the *Shakha Pramukh* sign a paper that he would guarantee that the employer paid compensation to the boy. The *Shakha Pramukh* personally accompanied the employer for the payment of the first instalment.

The status of litigants is also taken into account in the sense that the relevance of the litigants to the *Pramukh*s' or the party's interests is given weight. In another case, a *Shakha Pramukh* ruled that a contractor had to pay the wages agreed upon to the workers he had employed for a specific construction site although he himself had been paid less than he had calculated by the builder. This decision might have related to the fact that the workers all came from a slum pocket in Mumbai that the *Shakha Pramukh* patronised as a Municipal corporator; alienating them might have meant losing their votes. In a way, the *Shakha Pramukh* by his ruling circumvented the control of the contractor and established a direct patronage towards the workers of the area.

Shifts in normative positions are thus closely related to local relations of power and dependent on the individual *Shakha Pramukh's* social networks and local aspirations. His interest in votes or popular support are potentially opposed to his interests in possible 'donations' or payment of services from entrepreneurs. Such funds can, however, serve to buy votes or pay them off in kind. Thus, a *Shakha Pramukh* has to calculate whether he will gain more public support by using entrepreneurial funds to finance infrastructural projects, or by taking up the causes of the voters in their disputes with those who possibly would provide the funds.

Thus, the dominance of the *Shiv Sena*'s institutions over the operative legal order is precarious. It constantly has to adapt to the normative claims of its competitors. Its strategies relate to the specific rules of competition within the field of local governance. However, the competition over normative control is not equal; the rules that have evolved privilege those that are better equipped to form cooperative relations with the state agencies.

## Re-entering the State

The operative legal order thus generated in the practices and interactions of the various agencies active in the field of law and order in Mumbai's neighbourhoods is not 'outside' the state legal system. It is not in opposition to, autonomous of, or soon to be replaced or circumscribed by state law. Rather it is part of a regime of governance that also involves state institutions in a division of labour regarding control, allocation and adjudication. Its plural character derives from the specific rules of competition within this regime of governance, rules that open it up to constant contestations, but that also privilege some forms of contestations and limit the chances of others.

The interpretations of law, of the proper order and of specific legal institutions that are produced in the practices of various non-state organisations that administer adjudication to be endorsed and incorporated by the state agencies. 'Capturing' the state, or entering it via cooperative or complementary relations with individual state agencies is still the most successful strategy to dominate the field of local governance. Partly related to this intent of 'capturing the state', partly resulting from the state agencies' efforts to delegate particular tasks or simply to shed parts of their workload, the institutional integration between non-state actors and state agencies is intricate.

The *Shiv Sena* in particular has achieved a degree of institutional incorporation into state modes of governance that means that its interpretations and enactments of law are (re-) introduced into the practices of state agencies. While other agencies do often operate in a parallel, oppositional or hierarchical relation with the state agencies, it appears that the character of the institutional integration of the *Shiv Sena* with some, although not all state agencies is one of various degrees of cooperation and complementarity, and thus of mutual interdependence.

This becomes particularly evident in the cooperation between the police and the *Shiv Sena*. This involves the explicit delegation of tasks to the *Shiv Sena* and thus the implicit 'officialisation' of its practices and the norms effective therein. This is immediately relevant to the transformation of the operative legal order.

In most areas of the city the police are addressed in many disputes. These range from family disputes (between mother and daughter-in-law, between father and son, between brothers, between spouses), to quarrels over water taps or other public facilities, financial transactions that have gone wrong, fraud and violence. Every police station has to deal with a large number of complaints every day. They are registered either as non-cognisable offences or as cognisable offenses, and the form of registration is often an issue of local politics.[15]

In some areas the police delegates the resolution of these disputes to the *Shakhas*: "If you want to solve anything with the police you have to be with the *Shakha*. The police will send you to the *Shakha*," explained a Muslim resident of Dharavi. As Madhokar Sarpotdar, a prominent *Shiv Sena* leader, explained: "Some people go to the police, some go to the *Shakha*. We then cooperate with the police," and he was echoed by many of his fellow *Shakha Pramukh*s. Some of the police likewise cooperate with the *Pramukh*s. For many it was simply a way of getting rid of some of their workload. For others it was acceptance of their dependence on the local control the *Shiv Sena Shakha* might wield in an area. Others approve more fundamentally of such cooperative relations with the party. They feel legitimised, as former Police Commissioner Tyagi[16] put the matter in an interview, by the new policy of "community policing like in America."

Thus, in many areas there is no way around the *Shakha* for local disputes as the immediate, always accessible and largely cost-free agency of the state, the police delegates their resolution to the likewise immediate, always accessible and largely cheap *Shakha* jurisdiction.

---

[15] Sometimes registering a cognisable offense as a non-cognisable offense relieves the police of the work that is necessarily involved in the investigation into a cognisable offense. However, many a non-cognisable offense is converted into a cognisable one by the parties, either through a process of escalation of a dispute, or by representing a matter in a way that forces the police to take action. (Eckert 2002).

[16] Ramdeo Tyagi was charged in 2002 with shooting dead unarmed Muslim boys during the Bombay riots in 1992. He had previously joined the *Shiv Sena* as party member.

It is not simply in matters of dispute regulation that the police delegate work to the *Shakhas*. In administering the local system of 'illegality' the police frequently co-operate with the *Shakhas* and rely on the party's executive powers. The various constellations of 'illegality' present in the so-called informal economy of the city are 'supervised' by the *Shakhas*: tenure rights are controlled, permits are granted, checks are placed on certain activities, and access to municipal offices and to official licenses are organised by the *Pramukhs*. Thus, law and order, as well as the system of fines and licenses, 'taxes for the poor', are often administered by the police and the *Shakhas* in cooperation.

These daily instances of complementation are accompanied by regular non-intervention of the police in the illegal activities of the *Shiv Sena*. This is the most publicised form of cooperation, or 'devolution by default'.

In minor cases, someone who wishes to appeal to a state court against a ruling by a *Shakha* court, or to sue for a *Shakha*'s activities is faced with serious obstacles. Not only does the *Shiv Sena* have efficient and violent ways of imposing their rulings, but also judgments against the *Shiv Sena* and its members have been rarely given and even more rarely enforced. This is true especially for the more political rather than the purely economic illegal activities of the party. While some cases arising from economic activities, like the shoot-outs between various local leaders over territory, or the real-estate cases *Shiv Sena* members have been involved in, sometimes lead to convictions, the cases of agitation, rioting or incitement of hatred[17] are mostly inconclusive. Many of them are pending, and many somehow or other lapse.

Often the lack of legal sanction against clearly illegal activities of the *Shiv Sena* starts with police failure to register, prevent or investigate acts of members of the party. The initial explanation of police inaction is frequently that such action would lead to the escalation of violence. It is a preventive caution, a fear of arousing Bal Thackeray's anger and threats of escalation. Additional Commissioner of Police V.N. Deshmukh revealed an instance in his deposition before the Srikrishna commission. This said that, despite the speeches of Bal Thackeray and other *Sena* leaders being actionable at law, no action was taken against them because of previous police experience that, whenever *Sena* leaders were arrested, *bandhs* and violence followed.

---

[17] These cases relate usually to Section 153 (A) of the Indian Penal Code forbidding the promotion of enmity between groups on grounds of religion, race, place of birth and residence.

"The anticipated consequences were a deterrent to taking preventive action against leaders of the *Shiv Sena*".[18]

However, judicial inaction against the *Shiv Sena* as well as judicial bias in favour of it becomes particularly apparent in the judgments passed against *Sainiks*. Hansen reports how sentences for rioting in Maharashtrian villages against *Sainiks* and Muslim youths differed vastly in severity (Hansen 1998: 59-60).

The Srikrishna Commission's ineffectiveness is possibly the most extreme example of the immunity given to the *Shiv Sena*. While the commission held the party and its leaders responsible for the 1993 riots in Mumbai (Srikrishna Commission Report 1998), its findings were not admitted as legal evidence and its indictment did not have any legal, let alone other consequences for those indicted. In 2000 the Supreme Court ordered the government of Maharashtra to open criminal investigations, but not against the *Shiv Sena*. Only the police officers indicted by the report were charged with atrocities and investigated.[19]

There are, thus, strategies of delegation, like the every-day delegation of dispute resolution by the police to the *Shakhas* or the delegation of administrative control over the local economy. There are also strategies of default or avoidance, like the inaction towards the *Shiv Sena*'s minor and major criminal activities. These strategies together permanently change the operative legal order. Both are part of a system of division of labour that has evolved through the mutual usefulness of the unrelated strategies of individual organisations.

---

[18] Reported in *The Afternoon*, 24.2.1997, p.8

[19] The attempts by members of the NCP to convict Bal Thackeray failed. Thomas Hansen considers the commission an instrument for the upkeep of the facade of the state's neutrality (Hansen 2001). In fact, the frequent use of judicial commissions of enquiry, and their status, seem to relate to the state's idea of the encompassing state and the republic. However, the fact that such commissions are regularly rather ineffectual, and that their status is by definition not judicial, has the paradoxical effect that the performance makes all the more visible the fact that it is all a mere facade. The function of a facade to pose as something more than a facade is undermined by the obvious facade-nature of the commissions. Thus, the facade of the encompassing state facading the selective state is increasingly abandoned, thus shifting legitimacy and legality towards the latter's practices.

What is of interest for the emergence of new forms of legal pluralism is firstly that the legal order is changed by the *Shiv Sena* dominating adjudicative and regulative practices. This occurs because it is the institution to which various state agencies delegate tasks, and its activities are rarely hindered. Hence it can dominate or even monopolise local governance. Secondly, however, the operative legal order is changed beyond this, because the immunity awarded to the *Shiv Sena*'s activities generally shifts the delimitation of legality and legitimacy within the public space. Decisive is not simply the ability of the *Shiv Sena* to practise freely its visions of normative order and to impose them to a large degree on the local context. Also important is the fact that situations created by the *Shiv Sena*'s activities and their subsequent toleration as factual entail a possibly permanent shift in the norms of legality and legitimacy. The immunity awarded to the *Shiv Sena* treats activities that are officially denoted illegal as if they were legal, or at least legitimate. They become imbued with the 'normativity of the factual' and thus guide action and expectations: the rules of the game have changed.

Neither the practices of delegation nor those of default are necessarily due to an integrated strategy on the part of the government or 'the powers that be'. Rather they arise from complex situational processes of avoidance and instrumentalisation. Delegation to the *Shiv Sena Shakhas* is often a result of the attempt to shed workload; immunity is sometimes awarded because of fear of escalation. However, at the same time the party's activities have been useful to or made use of for the purposes of other organisations.

There are manyfold instrumentalisations of the *Shiv Sena*'s activities for other ends. Such are the Congress party's in its struggle against the communist unions of Bombay once upon a time (Ribeiro 1998: 116-117, 217; Gupta 1982: 176; Purandare 1999: 67); the BJP's in its symbiotic relationship with the party (Hansen 1998; Eckert 2003: 159); those of industrial management on the local level (Gupta 1982: 176-177; Eckert 2003: 193); or those of different state agencies, like the police or some of the municipal offices. These instrumentalisations promote also the dominance of the *Shiv Sena* in local governance and the changes in the operative legal order. Thus, although within these alliances of governance individual actors and organisations have their own agendas, and although these are often unrelated to each other and possibly even contradictory to a degree, the aggregation of their strategies, and their collaboration or cooperation creates a tendency that is clear in direction. These implicit and instrumental alliances and quasi-circumstantial cases of co-operation inserted new norms into the practices of state agencies and the operative legal order, thus shifting the norms and rules of legitimate action.

## Between monopolisation and pluralisation

Studies of legal pluralism have stressed how the rules operative in different semi-autonomous social fields are constituted by the interaction, mutual influence and situational use of state and non-state legal orders (Moore 1973; K. v. Benda-Beckmann 1981; Fitzpatrick 1983). State law is, however, often treated not as semi-autonomous but (implicitly) as autonomous, as shaping but not as being shaped. Moore, for example, when elaborating on her idea of the semi-autonomous social field mentions that state law might be affected (Moore 1973: 745) but she shows only how it is part of the operative 'rules of the game' (Moore 1973: 743). However, as the case of the *Shiv Sena* seems to indicate, state law is fundamentally transformed by the productions of legal order in the interactions of various actors involved in the administration of law and order. In the case of Mumbai, too, state law is constitutive of the rules of the game. However, looking at the local establishment of the *Shiv Sena* it becomes clear that organisations that are involved in governmental tasks, be they administrative, charitable, judicial or others, transform the operative legal order. Not only is the relation between productive, distributive, regulative and legislative tasks more intricate than currently fashionable policies of subsidiarity assume. Law is generated in practices that are formally not concerned with legislation. The 'laws' generated in organisational practices become part of the operative legal order and are, through the interaction of these institutions, re-introduced into the practices of state agencies and thus enter, via practice rather than legislation, the state legal order.

The informal devolution of judicial tasks has the paradoxical effect that it triggers the 'capture of the state' by those non-governmental organisations that have posed as alternatives to the state, by the entry into state practices of their particular versions of law. At the same time this 'capture' of the state triggered by de-étatisation is structured in its means by state law which inadvertently forces the 'captors' to adhere to the demands and ideas of law brought into the fray by their clients. This produces a specific form and determines specific means of competition, not abolishing other possible means but limiting them within the confines of existing alternatives.

Hence, on the one hand, the state and state law are central as they are to be occupied, to be captured, to be the vehicle of a particular normative vision. On the other hand the state and state law are central in that they still structure the terms through which non-state actors introduce their norms into state practice, as well as the conditions within which they act and compete with each other.

What is at issue is thus the production of a relatively integrated operative legal order in the interactions of various actors involved in the field of regulation and adjudication. This distinguishes these processes of legal pluralism from situations where distinct sets of law operate in competition with or in subsidiary relation to one another.

These processes of the establishment and adaptation of unnamed law shed light on the complex matters of the use and transformation of law and the precariousness of power relations. The fact that an organisation like the *Shiv Sena,* that has obtained a considerable degree of regulatory autonomy and powers of implementation, is still bound to the offers of its competitors (among them the state) of normative and legal interpretations, highlights the conditions under which an operative legal order is shaped by plural pressures. The operative legal order is thus a conglomerate of competing versions, swaying between the monopolisation of a single version and processes of pluralisation.

Thus, if we consider state law and non-state law as constitutive of each other we need still to look at the particular constitutive processes of a legal order, i.e. at the processes that produce, re-produce and/or transform it. Different processes of interaction, of mutual impact, and of various modes of 'devolution' and 'appropriation' have different results regarding the questions of who are the social actors involved in encoding the content of legal plurality are. They also have different results regarding the shape of legal pluralism itself. They differ as to the degrees of pluralisation or homogenisation, the nature of the borders between various 'sets of law', and between different semi-autonomous social fields, they differ in the ways these borders are drawn and by whom.

Fitzpatrick's notion of 'combined law' (Fitzpatrick 1983: 168) draws attention to the plurality of *interactions* between various actors that are involved in shaping the 'combined' legal institutions. He focuses on the analysis of the history of the establishment of these institutions, the precise processes of 'combining' that shape an operative legal order. Both the transformation as well as the preservation of an operative legal order, its pluralisation as well as its homogenisation, are dynamic processes resulting from social, political and economic struggles.

It can be argued that the resulting situation of legal pluralism is a function of the power relations of a particular society at a particular point in time. Specific constellations of legal pluralism have often been considered to be congruent with and determined by elite interests, and "probably functional to the power structures of ... society" (Santos 1995: 236). The Indian state, too, has been seen as the expression of the power relations between specific dominant groups or classes (Bardhan 1984; Vanaik 1990). The story of the emergence of the dominance of local governance by organisations like the *Shiv Sena*, however, can be told in two apparently contradictory ways: either as the story of the (cunning) engagement of the 'elites' in shaping a particular constellation of legal pluralism and *devolving* local control to organisations like the *Shiv Sena* (e.g. Brass 1997); or as the story of the 'failure of governance' (Sen Gupta 1996; Chopra 1996) where a local organisation has *appropriated* the powers of the state, its monopoly of coercive force and of law, as many of the analyses of the demise of the Nehruvian developmental state would hold. (It can be told also as the story that the failure of governance is in fact a strategy of cunning: Randeria 2002). But both seem to be the case. The evident strategies of instrumentalisation, avoidance and default towards the activities of the *Shiv Sena* created opportunities for the dominance or even monopolisation of local modes of governance. The shifts in the relations of power and in the norms of public space are, thus, possibly more fundamental than could be attributed to connivance. They are due to the particular use made of the opportunities created in the aggregation of the strategies of instrumentalisation and default, and thus a product of the merger of cunning devolution and forceful appropriation.

# References

AGNES, Flavia
1995    'Redefining the agenda of the women's movement within a secular framework.' Pp. 136-157 in Urvashi Butalia and Tanika Sarkar (eds.).
BARDHAN, Pradab
1984    *The Political Economy of Development in India*. Oxford: Blackwell.
BAXI, Upendra
1992    'People's law, development and justice.' Pp. 97-114, in: Csaba Varga (ed.), *Comparative Legal Cultures*. Aldershot: Dartmouth.
BENDA-BECKMANN, Franz von
1992    'Changing legal pluralism in Indonesia.' *Yuridika* 8(4): 1 -23.

BENDA-BECKMANN, Keebet von

1981    'Forum shopping and shopping forums: dispute processing in a Minangkabau village in West Sumatra.' *Journal of Legal Pluralism* 19: 117-139.

2001    'Transnational dimensions of legal pluralism.' Pp. 33-48 in Wolfgang Fikentscher (ed.), *Begegnung und Konflikt - eine kulturanthropologische Bestandaufnahme*. Munich: C.H. Beck.

BRASS, Paul

1997    *Theft of an Idol. Text and Context in the Representation of Collective Violence*. Princeton: Princeton University Press.

BUTALIA, Urvashi

1995    'Muslims and Hindus, men and women: communal stereotypes and the partition of India.' Pp. 58-81 in Urvashi Butalia and Tanika Sarkar (eds.).

BUTALIA, Urvashi and Tanika SARKAR (eds.)

1995    *Women and the Hindu Right: A Collection of Essays*. New Delhi: Kali for Women.

CHANDAVARKAR, Rajnarayan

1981    'Worker's politics and the mill districts in Bombay between the wars.' *Modern Asian Studies* 15(3): 603-647.

1994    *The Origins of Industrial Capitalism in India; Business Strategies and the Working Classes in Bombay, 1900-1940*, Cambridge: Cambridge University Press.

1998    *Imperial Power and Popular Politics; Class Resistance and the State in India 1850-1950*, Cambridge: Cambridge University Press.

CHOPRA, Vir

1996    'The mirage of good governance.' *Politics India*: 24-28.

COHN, Bernard

1959    'Some notes on law and change in Northern India.' *Economic Development and Cultural Change* 8: 79-93.

ECKERT, Julia

2002    'Policing Mumbai.' Unpublished manuscript.

2003    *The Charisma of Direct Action; Power, Politics and the* Shiv Sena. Delhi: Oxford University Press.

FITZPATRICK, Peter

1983    'Law, plurality, and underdevelopment.' Pp. 159-182 in David Sugarman (ed.), *Legality, Ideology and the State*. London: Academic Press.

GALANTER, Marc (with Upendra BAXI)
1997    'Panchayat Justice: An Indian experiment in legal access.' Pp. 54-91 in
        Marc Galanter (ed.), *Law and Society in Modern India*. Delhi, Oxford:
        Oxford University Press.
GALANTER, Marc and Jayant KRISHNAN
2002    'Debased informalism: Lok Adalats and legal rights in modern India.' Paper
        presented at the panel *The Reach of Law in India* at the Conference of the
        Law and Society Association, Vancouver.
GUPTA, Dipankar
1982    *Nativism in a Metropolis: The Shiv Sena in Bombay*, Delhi: Manohar.
HANSEN, Thomas Blom
1998    *Hinterland Hindutva*. Unpublished manuscript, Roskilde.
2001    'Governance and myths of state in Mumbai.' Pp. 31-67 in Chris Fuller and
        John Harris (eds.), *The Everyday State and Society in India*. Delhi: Oxford
        University Press.
HENSMAN, Rohini
2001    *The Impact of Globalisation on Employment in India and Responses from the
        Formal and Informal Sectors,* Working Paper, No. 15. Amsterdam:
        CLARA.
HUMPHREY, Caroline
1999    'Russian protection rackets and the appropriation of law and order.' Pp.
        199-232 in Josiah Heyman (ed.), *States and Illegal Practices*. Oxford: Berg.
KOLFF, D.H.A.
1992    'The Indian and the British law machines; some remarks on law and society
        in British India.' Pp. 201-236 in Wolfgang J. Mommsen and Jaap de Moor
        (eds.), *European Expansion and Law*. Oxford: Berg.
LIKOSKY, Michael (ed.)
2002    *Transnational Legal Processes: Globalisation and Power Disparities*,
        London: Butterworths.
MOORE, Sally Falk
1973    'Law and social change: the semi-autonomous social field as an appropriate
        subject of study.' *Law and Society Review*: 719-746.
PANWALKAR, Pratima
1998    'Slum Ökonomie in Dharavi.' *Stadtbauwelt* 48: 2640-2645.
PURANDARE, Vaibhav
1999    *The Sena Story*, Mumbai: Business Publications Inc.

RANDERIA, Shalini
2002    'Glocalisation of law: environmental justice, World Bank, NGOs and the cunning state in India.' Paper presented at the conference *Mobile People, Mobile Law*. Max Planck Institute for Social Anthropology, Halle/Saale.

RIBEIRO, Julio
1998    *Bullet for Bullet: My Life as a Police Officer*, New Delhi: Viking.

RISSE, Thomas, Stephen C ROPP and Kathryn SIKKINK
1999    *The Power of Human Rights: International Norms and Domestic Change*, Cambridge: Cambridge University Press.

SANTOS, Boaventura de Sousa
1995    *Towards a New Common Sense; Law, Science and Politics in the Paradigmatic Transition*. New York, London: Routledge.

SCHLICHTE, Klaus, and Boris WILKE
2000    'Der Staat und einige seiner Zeitgenossen.' *Zeitschrift für Internationale Beziehungen* 2: 359-384.

SEN GUPTA, Bhabani
1996    *Problems of Governance*. New Delhi: Konark Publishers.

SETALVAD, Teesta
1995    'The Woman Shiv Sainik and her Sister Swayamsevika.' Pp. 233-244 in Urvashi Butalia and Tanika Sarkar (eds.).

SRIKRISHNA COMMISSION REPORT
1998    Mumbai: Jyoti Punwani, Vrijendra.

STRANGE, Susan
1996    *The Retreat of the State. The Diffusion of Power in the World Economy*, Cambridge: Cambridge University Press.

TROTHA, Trutz von
2000    'Die Zukunft liegt in Afrika: Vom Zerfall des Staates.' *Leviathan* 2000/2: 253-279.

VANAIK, Achin
1990    *The Painful Transition: Bourgeois Democracy in India*. London: Verso.

VOLKOV, Vadim
2000    'Gewaltunternehmer im postkommunistischen Russland.' *Leviathan* 2000/2: 173-191.

WHITSON, Sarah Leah
1992    'Neither fish, nor flesh, nor good red herring. Lok Adalats: an experiment in informal dispute resolution in India.' *Hastings International and Comparative Law Review* 15: 391- 445.

WORLD BANK
2000    *India: Policies to Reduce Poverty and Accelerate Sustainable Development.*
        Washington DC: World Bank.

# GLOBALIZATION, STATE LAW AND LEGAL PLURALISM IN BRAZIL

Arnaldo Moraes Godoy

This paper deals with the relation between globalization, State law and legal pluralism in the Brazilian context. It assumes that there is tendency which simultaneously increases and reduces the power of the traditional State, depending on the aspect of peripheral politics which is taken into account, thereby opening a gap which has been filled by legal pluralism.

Globalization surprises, enchants, scares (Lyotard 1999: 37), somehow implementing several forms of alienation, to adopt Marx's concepts. Globalization surprises us by the velocity with which it rearticulates our lives. Globalization enchants us with the promises that it brings, proclaiming a world free of poverty. Globalization scares us, for it shows the actual circumstances in which we can recognize our boundless fallibility.

From an economic standpoint one could admit in Globalization the triumph of the market. Such perception indicates an explicit pragmatism, a subtle rationalism, as if globalization would be the only vehicle to progress. But globalization is also a discursive practice and in that sense its supporters develop an appropriation of History in order to justify their truths. I mention presentism, a way of looking to the past as the key to the present, with today's eyes, performing a radical subjectivity (Schaff 1995: 111).

Globalization may be seen as the consequence of a process of evolution, if one adopts the so-called historical approach. There is a tendency to manipulate History, taking from the old times only what makes sense to our days, as Walter

Benjamin suggested with the image of the tiger's leap into the past (Benjamin 1985: 261). Within this same cultural milieu, Francis Fukuyama announced the end of History and the twilight of the last man (Fukuyama 1992). With the apparent victory of democracy and neoliberalism, especially after the collapse of the Berlin wall, all the utopias are gone, still according to Fukuyama. From the Hegelian philosophy, which also recognized the end of History, and from its historiographical tradition, as appropriated by Marx, for whom History would come to an end with the dictatorship of proletariat, Francis Fukuyama set the epistemological anchors of his theory. Fukuyama took Marxist tools to combat Marx himself. The end of History would not be the dictatorship of proletariat, for the end of History would be the dictatorship of the market.

Globalization has been also understood with suspicion.   Michael Hardt and Antonio Negri brought us the concept of Empire (Hardt and Negri 2001), as a formulation of political power in a globalized world. Empire would be different from Imperialism. The latter has been subject to a permanent state of war, an endless conflict among the nations. The former would be an hierarchical structure capable of incorporating the United States, the European Union, Japan, the big international corporations, and other protagonists of political power under the guise of 'global players', as for instance the IMF and the WTO. According to Hardt and Negri, Empire would be a sovereign power which would govern the world (Hardt and Negri 2001: xi). The United States would have an important position in this web: the Americans would have the police power in this new world order. The contemporary wars the world has faced could confirm this image. Today's wars are fought under the flag of *just wars*.

Globalization and its intellectual counterpart, liberalism, are also the target of some criticism from Roberto Mangabeira Unger, a Brazilian scholar and political activist who teaches at Harvard. For Unger, liberalism is the guard who watches over us as over a prison-house (Unger 1984: 3). Globalization would be a euphemism for Americanization (Unger 1984: xxxviii). Unger has a radical project, an alternative to Marxism, to social democracy and to neoliberalism. Unger insists that his political project is not a third way, as for instance conceived by Anthony Giddens (2001), Unger's project is a second way, softened or not, given the fact that there is only one alternative presently offered to the world (Unger 1984: xviii). Unger defends what he names an empowerment to democracy, the radicalization of a concrete and constructive popular participation, fighting all the given patterns, imbued with determinism, which enchain us under the rules that enforce the abstract idea of market.

Globalization is theoretically centered on neoliberalism as a herald of the power of the market (Boxberger and Klimenta 1999: 9), in spite of much criticism within the mainstream itself, as suggested by Joseph Stiglitz (Stiglitz 2002: 23). Globalization and neoliberalism demand a cluster of economic reforms in the international scenario (Chossudovsky 1999: 11). Empire manipulates the global players, such as the IMF and the World Bank, in order to guarantee optimal conditions for the development of the capitalism that it defends, centered in the perceptions of freedom (Friedman 2002: 22), of criticism of totalitarianism (Hayek 1994: 199), and of dichotomies between capitalism and socialism (Schumpeter 1975: 232), as if human society were the result of a mere association of people seeking mutual cooperation.

The world lives a perennial crisis of financial instability. International competition demands a relation between capital and work within the frame of the cheap labor force. Pressured and monitored by the IMF and its programs, the Nation States are under a demand to increase their tax burdens and to decrease the amount of social service which they are presumptively obliged to render. This is the curse of the fiscal crisis. There is also a structural crisis which affects the governability of the Nation State. The neoliberal political agenda has the effect of separating the State from its citizens, especially within the South American context. The endless search for monetary stability is the goal which moves the conservative forces. Brazil exemplifies quite well this situation.

In South America traditional law has been under assault as a consequence of globalization. In Brazil this can be easily seen if one considers the various branches of normativity, such as Constitutional Law, Administrative Law, Labor Law, Tax Law, Procedural Law, Consumer Law and Environmental Law.

Constitutional Law is the main target which the forces of globalization are trying to hit. Because there is a widespread assumption that the Nation State has to be immediately changed, all the Brazilian Constitutional conquests are under siege. Citizenship and its actual meaning is a concept that lacks operability in Brazilian daily life. The disenchantment with the left wing government is a manifestation of this perception. There is a common belief that the State is no longer able to provide justice or security. The constitutional text has become a mere symbol, as the flag or the national anthem. The entirety of the fundamental rights that the Brazilian constitution had assured, typical in an old-fashioned Welfare State, are no longer provided, as a result of the diminution of the State and its traditional responsibilities.

Recently Brazil underwent a constitutional reform, brought about by several constitutional amendments. The main function of these was the reformulation of the traditional state under the pressures of globalization forces. The Brazilian economy has been opened to international capital. Under the command of the IMF 'shadow program', the main features of the present scenario are the liberalization of prices, the collapse of State investment, the liberalization of trade, structural reforms, the divestiture and privatization of State enterprises and land tenure, and the privatization of agricultural land.

Telecommunications, gas and petroleum exploitation, banking, the whole economy has been opened to international operations and interests. For instance, social security has also undergone extensive normative changes, especially as to the minimum age of retirement.

Constitutional Amendment No. 5, from 1995, provided that "the states shall have the power to operate, directly or by means of concession, the local services of piped gas, as provided for by law, it being forbidden to issue any provisional measure for its regulation", thus ending the monopoly of the State over the distribution of piped gas. Constitutional Amendment No. 6, from 1995, ended the monopoly of Brazilian companies over the prospecting and mining of mineral resources. Constitutional Amendment No. 7, from 1995, ended the predominance of domestic ship owners and ships with the Brazilian flag and registration, related to the regulation of air, ocean and ground transportation. Constitutional Amendment No. 8, from 1995, ended the state monopoly of telecommunications services. Constitutional Amendment No. 9, also from 1995, ended the state monopoly of the supply of petroleum, as well as the conditions for contracting the distribution of gas.

Administrative Law has effected a reformulation of the traditional role of the State. Aside from a massive selling of the public enterprises (in the fields of communication, transportation and banking), there is a widespread tendency towards the multiplication of regulatory agencies, a juridical feature which in Brazil was unfamiliar until recently and which has somehow been copied from the North-American agencies.

Labor Law has witnessed a social dumping which was never seen before. Under the flag of 'flexibility of labor rules' there is a marked diminution of social and labor rights, some of which, such as the minimum wage and the limitation on working hours, were the achievements of years of struggle. The Brazilian Constitution has been criticized for the many labor rights it seeks to assure, such as the protection of employment against arbitrary dismissal or dismissal without just cause, unemployment insurance against involuntary unemployment, a severance-pay fund, and a nationally unified minimum monthly wage, established by law, capable of satisfying workers' basic needs and those of their families in respect of housing, food, education, health, leisure, clothing, hygiene, transportation and social security, with periodical adjustments to maintain its purchasing power. All these rules are purely rhetorical.

Tax Law has seen the enlargement of the State presence with the consequent increase in the national tax burden. There is a general increase in the tax rates as well as the creation of new taxes, related to income and to financial transactions. There is a general tax reform under way. Indirect taxation has been dramatically increased and as the outcome the actual tax burden is concentrated on the shoulders of the have nots, who pay the same rates as the better off.

Procedural Law is demanding new forms of operability, as a result of the general use of the internet and of other cybernetic resources. There is also an emergence of collective rights, as opposed to individual rights, which are the main features of a law system still imbued with Roman law. The judiciary has a heavy load of cases to decide. Forensic services are very expensive in all categories, from court fees to those of lawyers. Recent denunciations of corruption have also helped to increase the distrust that people have towards the judiciary.

Civil Law faces a myriad of new problems, from bioethics to virtual contracts, from new models of marriage to cybernetic infidelity, as well as the apparent confusion between public and private spheres. A new form of judicial person is on the rise, in the form of the NGO, the non governmental organizations.

Consumer Law tries to shape a new pattern of citizenship, whose main feature would be based on consumption power. However, because of the social inequalities in Brazil, that model of citizenship is reserved to a small proportion of the country's population.

Environmental Law tends to oppose the Economy to Ecology, making the latter a hostage to the concept of sustainable development. Albeit the Brazilian Constitution indicates that

> all have the right to an ecologically balanced environment, which is an asset of common use and essential to a healthy quality of life, and both the Government and the community shall have the duty to defend and preserve it for present and future generations,

what one sees in reality is the degradation of the natural resources of Brazil, especially in the rain forest and in the overpopulated urban areas such as Sao Paulo and Rio de Janeiro.

The present, general lack of confidence in the State and the legal rules it tries to enforce brings to reality the

> theoretical possibility of more than one legal order within one social-political space, based on different sources of ultimate validity and maintained by forms of organization other than the State (Benda-Beckmann 2003: 275),

that is to say, legal pluralism, in spite of the State law's claims to integrity, coherence and uniformity (Griffiths 2002: 296). Whatever the theoretical debates around a definition of legal pluralism, either as a non-state law recognized by the state, or as a non-state law independent of recognition, Brazilian social reality pragmatically confirms the existence of many layers of normative power, outside the state and far beyond the perception of *asphalt law*, as announced by Santos (1995).

The increase in the drug business as well as the growth of corruption have dramatically changed the reality of the sites visited by Santos when he did his research in Brazil in the 1970s. If one were to visit *Pasargada* today (as Santos named the *favela* he studied), one would find a totally different normative reality. This provides a negative feature of legal pluralism, as depicted by Santi Romano, an Italian law professor who described the *mafia* as a source of legal power, in the early days of theorization about legal pluralism. It is about time to revisit *Pasargada*.

Within the Brazilian state, the coexistence of many sources of normative power transcends Woodman's idea, for whom there can be no map of law (Woodman 2003: 383), albeit it must be well understood that legal pluralism in this context exists within a major state order, that is, legal pluralism in a weak sense, as also defined by Woodman (2003).

The general distrust towards the new Brazilian state as shaped by globalization is the main reason which determines people's drive to new patterns of power, in order to solve conflicts of daily life. Because solutions to real problems can be achieved outside the traditional domain of the State, there is indeed a contemporary tendency to promote the utilization of alternative sources of dispute resolution, as a result of the weakness of the State. Therefore there is an unexpected relationship between globalization, State law and legal pluralism in Brazil, which tends to increase as the globalization of poverty continues apace.

# References

BENDA-BECKMANN, Franz von
2003    'Who's Afraid of Legal Pluralism?' Pp. 275-298 in Rajendra Pradhan (ed.), *Legal Pluralism and Unofficial Law in Social, Economic and Political Development: Papers of the XIIIth International Congress of the Commission on Folk Law and Legal Pluralism*, Vol. III. Kathmandu: International Centre for the Study of Nature, Environment and Culture.
BENJAMIN, Walter
1968    *Illuminations*. New York: Schocken Books.
BOXBERGER, Gerald, and Harald KLIMENTA
1999    *As dez mentiras da globalização*. São Paulo: Aquariana, Tradução de Inês Antônio Lohbauer.
CHOSSUDOVSKY, Michel
1999    *A globalização da pobreza: impactos das reformas do FMI e do Banco Mundial*. São Paulo: Moderna.
COWEN, Tyler
2002    *Creative Destruction (How Globalization is Changing the World's Cultures)*. Princeton: Princeton University Press.
FRIEDMAN, Milton
2002    *Capitalism and Freedom*, 4th ed. Chicago and London: The University of Chicago Press.
FRIEDMAN, Thomas L.
2000    *The Lexus and the Olive Tree*. New York: Anchor Books.
FUKUYAMA, Francis
1992    *The End of History and the Last Man*. London: Penguin Books.

GIDDENS, Anthony
2001    *A terceira via: reflexões sobre o impasse político atual e o futuro da social-democracia* [translation of *The Third Way: The Renewal of Social Democracy*], 4th ed. Rio de Janeiro: Record.

GRIFFITHS, Anne
2002    'Legal Pluralism.' Pp. 289-311 in R. Banakar and M. Travers (eds.), *An Introduction to Law and Social Theory*. Oxford and Portland Oregon: Hart Publishing.

HABERMAS, Jürgen
1975    *Legitimation Crisis*. Boston: Beacon Press.

HARDT, Michael, and Antonio NEGRI
2001    *Empire,* 10th ed. Cambridge MA: Harvard University Press.

HAYEK, F.A
1994    *The road to serfdom*. 5th ed. Chicago: The University of Chicago Press.

HELD, David
1995    *Democracy and the Global Order: from the modern state to cosmopolitan governance*. Stanford: Stanford University Press.

HELD, David and Anthony MCGREW (eds.)
2003    *The global transformations reader: an introduction to the globalization debate,* 2nd ed. Cambridge, UK: Polity Press.

HIRST, Paul and Grahame THOMPSON
1998    *Globalização em questão: a economia internacional e as possibilidades de governabilidade*. Petrópolis: Ed. Vozes.

HUNTINGTON, Samuel P.
2003    *The Clash of Civilizations and the Remaking of World Order*. New York : Simon and Schuster.

JAMESON, Fredric
2001    *Postmodernism Or, The Cultural Logic of Late Capitalism.* Durham: Duke University Press.

LYOTARD, Jean-François
1999    *The Postmodern Condition: A Report on Knowledge*. Minneapolis: University of Minnesota Press.

RENTON, David (ed.)
2001    *Marx on Globalisation*. London: Lawrence & Wishart.

SANTOS, Boaventura de Sousa
1995    *Towards a New Common Sense: Law, Science and Politics in the Paradigmatic Transition*. New York and London: Routledge.

SCHAFF, Adam
1995    *História e verdade*, 6th ed. São Paulo: Martins Fontes.
SCHUMPETER, Joseph A.
1975    *Capitalism, Socialism and Democracy*. New York: Harper Perennial.
STIGLITZ, Joseph E.
2002    *Globalization and its Discontents*. New York and London: W.W. Norton
        & Company.
TOMLINSON, John
1999    *Globalization and Culture*. Chicago: The University of Chicago Press.
UNGER, Roberto Mangabeira
1977    *Law in Modern Society*. New York: The Free Press.
1984    *Knowledge and Politics*. London and New York: The Free Press.
1986    *The Critical Legal Studies Movement*. Cambridge: Harvard University
        Press.
2001    *False Necessity: Anti-Necessitarian Social Theory in the Service of
        Radical Democracy*. London and New York: Verso.
WALLERSTEIN, Immanuel
2000    *The essential Wallerstein*. New York: The New Press.
WOODMAN, Gordon
2003    'Why there can be no map of law.'  Pp. 383-392 in Rajendra Pradhan
        (ed.), *Legal Pluralism and Unofficial Law in Social, Economic and
        Political Development: Papers of the XIIIth International Congress of the
        Commission on Folk Law and Legal Pluralism*, Vol. III. Kathmandu:
        International Centre for the Study of Nature, Environment and Culture.
YERGIN, Daniel, and Joseph STANISLAW
1998    *The Commanding Heights*. New York: Touchstone.
ZOLO, Danilo
1997    *Cosmopolis - Prospects for World Government*. Cambridge : Polity Press.

# RELATIONSHIPS BETWEEN RESOURCE GOVERNANCE AND RESOURCE CONFLICT: NEPALESE EXPERIENCES

Bishnu Raj Upreti

## 1. Introduction

In this paper I am attempting to highlight the relationship between resource governance, resource scarcity, and conflict in Nepal. The notion of resource governance is discussed to address environmental problems such as scarcity of natural resources and environmental services. Environmental governance, in this paper, refers to a principle, process and practices of mainstreaming environmental and ecological issues and concerns in policies, plans, laws and regulations, strategies, decisions and actual actions at different levels (Including the national level) within a good governance framework. This framework is consensus oriented, participatory, guided by the rule of law, effective and efficient, accountable and transparent, responsive, equitable and inclusive.

Conflict in this paper refers to observable differences in opinion, misunderstandings, clashes of interest, disagreements, complaints in public, protests by argument and physical assault, antipathy, and filing of cases with the local administration, police and courts (Upreti 2002). When the latitude of tolerance crosses the bottom line then conflict occurs. Feelings of unfairness, suspicion, injustice, mistrust and suchlike ultimately lead to conflict. Resource conflicts produce both positive and negative consequences and alter existing social relations (Buckels 1999). They induce change in resource management and utilisation, policy process, livelihood strategies, land and agriculture, gender relations, power structures, and individual and collective behaviour. In most cases the combined effect of some or many of such factors can either escalate or resolve a conflict (Upreti 1999).

The study of resource conflict involves investigating almost all aspects of human activity and interactivity ranging from the behaviour of individuals to group characteristics concerning governance of environmental services. Dominant thinking in conflict paradigms treats 'environmental and resources conflict' as a particular event in a particular point of time that needs to be resolved through legal and regulatory interventions. However, I perceive conflict as an inevitable process that can be used as a constructive means for social transformation and agrarian change. I prefer to use the term 'conflict management' instead of conflict resolution. Conflict management is making progress. On aspect of improving a conflict situation, progress may be developed in mutual gains, learning, achieving agreements, laying foundations for further negotiation or fully resolving conflict. Progress is a way of thinking about a conflict situation that recognises that conflict is inevitable and ongoing, and that management of the conflict comes from continual improvement in areas of substance and relationships (Daniels and Walker 1997). It is not always possible to fully resolve all environmental and resources conflicts but it is possible to manage them. Conflict resolution implies that conflict is totally resolved.

Conflict management basically focuses on negotiations about the use of resources. Conflict is also a source of learning[1] how to create opportunities for social change in society. When there is conflict it gives people opportunities to think, understand the causes of the problems, and look for solutions. Natural resource-conflict needs to be viewed in the wider context of historical, political, cultural, economic, institutional, organisational and technological dimensions that provide the basis for the creation, escalation, stalemate or management of conflicts. Therefore, resource conflict is interconnected with broader socio-political issues and their implications for environment, society and processes of agrarian change.

Land, forest and water are the most important resources for the economic

---

[1] Learning is a complex activity, which manifests itself in a change in people's behaviour. It is rooted in the human capacity to improve their understanding and skills on the basis of day-to-day experiences (Engel and Salomon 1997), external knowledge and surrounding environment.

development of Nepal. Conflict is common in the use and management of these resources. Therefore, management of conflict is crucial to achieve sustainable use and management of natural resources (Upreti 1999, 2001).

---

**Box 1**

Positive and Negative Outcomes of Conflict

Positive: Conflict can –

- motivate people to try harder – to win
- increase commitment, enhance group loyalty and spirit
- increase clarity about the problem and raise awareness
- lead to innovative breakthroughs and new approaches
- clarify underlying problems and facilitate change
- focus attention on basic issues and lead to solutions
- increase energy level, making visible key values
- sharpen approaches to agrarian reform and social change

Negative: Conflict can –

- lead to anger, avoidance, sniping, shouting, frustration, fear of failure, sense of personal inadequacy
- suppress critical information
- lower productivity by diverting effort to wasteful conflict
- sidetrack careers, ruin relationships
- disrupt patterns of work
- consume money and time
- escalate to violence, destroy social harmony, and lead to the collapse of society

---

In the context of natural resources the perceived inconsistencies in the allocation between people of acquired rights and incurred obligations, or contradictions between two or more jurisdictions lead to conflict. In the legal sense conflict management is the application of the laws and regulations to ensure rights and provide remedies that reconcile the inconsistencies and decide which systems are to govern particular cases (Oli, 1998).

## 2. Resource Scarcity as a Source of Present and Future Conflict

A Report of the Johns Hopkins Population Information Programme (JHPIP) highlights that nearly half a billion people worldwide are currently facing water shortages (JHPIP 1998). By 2025 one in every three people will live in countries short of water. At present 31 countries are facing water stress or water scarcity and by 2025 the number will have exploded fivefold. The World Water Forum (2000) also stresses that more than one billion people in the world have no access to water of sufficient quantity and quality to meet even a minimum level of health, income, safety and freedom from drudgery. The World's projected total of 8 billion people in 2025 will enormously increase pressure on natural resources and environmental services and may cause a catastrophe. The competition between industrial, urban, and agricultural use for natural resources is mounting and the per capita consumption of natural resources is increasing (JHPIP 1998). Regional conflicts over natural resources are brewing and could turn violent as shortages grow. In all continents and countries, people are already bickering over access to natural resources and competition for their use can be fiercer in the future. For example, serious conflicts are developing concerning large dams such as the Lesotho Highlands Water Project in the Malibamatso and Little Orange Rivers in Southern Africa funded by the World Bank. For such projects the World Bank is facing an onslaught of criticism not only over its support for big dams, but also for creating severe conflict in the host countries. As world water scarcity bites deeper into economies dependent on cheap water supplies, there is conflict over river catchments and lakes. Dams such as the Three Gorges Dam in China have become symbols of official tyranny, with whole cities being flooded and engineers being given free reign to resettle populations who are inconveniently living in river valleys (Ohlsson 1995). Because of the competition for available natural resources by an over-growing population, and resource capture by certain powerful people, the vital ecosystems on which humans and other species depend are severely threatened (World Water Forum 2000). The earth has lost 15% of its topsoil over the last 20 years through inappropriate agricultural practices. Water logging, salination and alkalisation affect another 1.5 million hectares of mostly irrigated agricultural land. Desertification and drought are severely limiting the production potential of the global agricultural system and posing several ecological challenges[2] (Röling 2000).

---

[2] See Beck et al., (1994) for details about future risks, problems and challenges to modern societies. Also see Lubchenco (1998) for challenges to science to achieve sustainable future environmental management.

Conflict between Egypt, Ethiopia and Sudan about the Nile with respect to flooding and water flow diversion, between Belgium and the Netherlands about the Maas and the Schelde with respect to salination and industrial pollution, between France, the Netherlands, Germany and Switzerland about the Rhine with respect to industrial pollution, between India and Bangladesh about the Brahmaputra and the Ganges with respect to siltation, flooding and water flow diversion, between Mexico and the USA about the Rio Grande and Colorado rivers with respect to salination, water flow and agrochemical pollution (Ohlsson 1995) are some examples to mention. Similarly, the conflicts such as those over the Amazonian, Borneo and Sumatran forests, the Massai forest, the Yellowstone National Parks, and also land disputes,[3] are all derived from political, economic or environmental motives. Internationally and domestically, the political wrangling and strife over natural resources are predicted to be one of the fundamental issues of the new millennium.

Globalisation is increasingly posing new challenges and creating new conflicts in Nepal. For example, the conflict between Article 27.3b of the Trade Related Aspects of Intellectual Property Rights (TRIPs) of the World Trade Organisation (WTO) and the Convention on Biological Diversity (CBD), increasing bio-piracy, uncertainties and threats caused by genetically modified organisms and terminator technology in the agricultural sector are all creating conflict.

If there is scarcity of resources, there is competition, so natural resources will be a continuous source of future conflict. In this context a few sentences of the speech delivered by Fidel Castro on the occasion of the 50th anniversary of the World Health Organisation is worth mentioning.

> The weather is changing, the seas and the atmosphere are heating up, the air and the water are polluted, the soil is eroding, the deserts are growing, the forest is disappearing, water is getting scarce. Who will save our species? The blind and uncontrollable

---

[3] The dispute between Israel and Palestine, the Kashmir land disputes, the grazing land dispute between the Tibetan autonomous region of China and Nepal, the Kalapani land dispute between Nepal and India, and land conflict between ethnic people and the white minority in Zimbabwe are just a few examples of land conflicts.

laws of the market? Neo-liberal globalisation? .... (Idris, 1998: 5).

## 3. Governance of Nepalese Natural Resources and Conflict

Population pressure, poverty, inequitable distribution and control, and bad governance are some of the root causes of conflict over natural resources and environment in Nepal. Land and forest resources are over-exploited because of heavy dependence of the ever-growing population (both human and animals). Resource scarcity is therefore directly linked with governance, accountability and transparency and a historically power-skewed socio-cultural legacy.

Water is one of the most important natural resources of Nepal. It is estimated that there are a total of 6000 rivers (CBS 1995). Despite the vast amount of water available, drinking water is scarce in many parts of the country. Industrial use of water in urban centres has created competition and conflict in inter- and intra-sectoral water use. Irrigation in mountain and hill regions, which constitute 83% of the Nepal's total area, is difficult because of steep slopes and the fragile geography, which causes recurring landslides and soil erosion. The growing population requires more food and growing more food requires more water. Physiographic characteristics and climatic factors affect such consumptive use of water but they vary spatially and seasonally. This leads to an unequal distribution. Nepalese water resource management is therefore characterised by an unjust and insufficient use of water, by contradiction and by conflicts. Water scarcity, competition and conflict are common features of social, economic, political and legal issues in Nepal (Upreti 2002).

Growing population, factories and farms all need more water and other natural resources. Competition between domestic consumption, industries, and farms is increasing and turning into disputes. Water pollution is another issue of conflict. We can see examples in Kathmandu Valley where the river systems are almost collapsing because the river-water is no longer useable. Conflict between the needs of populations living upstream of river basins and those dwelling downstream is mounting. Irrigation, a principal sector of water use in Nepal, intended to minimise the water scarcity in the field of agriculture, is creating its own conflicts and competition (Pradhan et al. 2000).

Forests are another important natural resource for economic and social development. Forest resources are one of the major resources directly contributing to the survival of rural people in Nepal. Forest resources directly fulfil forest-related subsistence needs of women, poor and backward people as well as commercial needs of well-off people. They provide inputs for agriculture and livestock, and supply medicinal herbs, timber and non-timber forest products. Forests also support irrigation, conserve watersheds, improve the condition of the soil, provide recreation for tourists through forest-based ecotourism and national parks and wildlife reserves, provide a habitat for flora and fauna and provide raw materials for the forest-based industries (Upreti 1999). Many of the agricultural production systems of the country are based directly or indirectly on forest resources. However, the Nepalese forests are severely threatened by political and commercial interests. In 1964 forests covered more than 45% of the total area of the country, and this had declined to 29% by 1998. It is reported that the forest area of Terai is being destroyed at the rate of 1.3% per year (NPC 1998: 290). Smuggling of forest products is posing another serious challenge. The productivity of the forest sector is decreasing due to uncontrolled migration and encroachment, smuggling, illegal hunting, grazing, forest fires, lack of scientific forest management, and poor political commitments and bureaucratic performance. Deforestation is resulting in an increasing loss of habitats for birds, wild animals and reptiles. IUCN has reported that 24 species of mammals, 9 species of reptiles, 27 species of birds, 2 species of insects and 13 species of plants have become endangered in Nepal (NPC 1998: 219).

The land use systems in Nepal are rapidly changing because of increased environmental consumerism through the information revolution, technological advancement, market intervention and globalisation processes. As a consequence, over-exploitation of natural resources and environmental services is becoming harsh reality. The lack of strong environmental governance, weak institutional arrangements and rapid globalisation are exerting enormous pressures on natural resources. Well-planned land use is one of the most important aspects of environmental governance to achieve economic and social development. If land is managed and used properly, according to its quality, type, capacity and physiographic characteristics, not only the agricultural productivity and other social and economic benefits can be increased but also environmental risks can be minimised (Upreti 2003).

Land is a crucial resource for the livelihood of Nepalese farmers. It is also a basis of feudalistic wealth and power. Due to the increasing human population and increasing numbers of unproductive livestock extreme pressure is being exerted on land resources (NPC 1998). Soil erosion, fertility decline, sedimentation and floods have degraded and continue to degrade the land. Causative factors of soil loss are steep slope cultivation, use of marginal land, overgrazing, forest fires, and population pressure.

Internal migration is rapidly increasing the population in urban centres and putting additional pressure on the urban environment. More than 90% of urban centres are located in the fertile agricultural areas. Huge quantities of land are used annually in building construction by government, semi-government, nongovernment and the private sectors (NPC 1998). The increasing pace of rural to urban migration is reducing the productivity of land in both rural and urban areas (HMG/N 1992). The government is not able to develop mutual links between rural and urban areas nor to provide equal opportunities in the rural areas. The regional imbalance, lack of infrastructure and employment opportunities and the unavailability of basic service facilities are the triggering factors for migration from rural to urban areas (NPC 1998). Land encroachment and unplanned settlements are the result of such migration whereby an imbalanced situation develops between men and land resources.

Skewed land distribution and gross disparities in land ownership are one of the major causes of poverty, injustice and social discrimination (Upreti 2000a). Because of such disparity, a large number of people have no access to productive land resources. More than 70% of farmers have less than one hectare of land (NPC 1998). Substantial regional variations in the distribution of agricultural lands exist in Nepal. The Terai Region occupies 17% of the total land area comprising 49% of the total agricultural land whereas the Hill Region covers 63% of the total land and accounts for 40% of agricultural land. Mountain Region occupies 20% of the total land with 11% of agricultural land. The Human Development Report-Nepal 1998 shows that the bottom 40% of agricultural households use only 9% of the total agricultural land owning on average less than 0.5 ha. The top 6% occupies more than 33% of the total. These inequalities are manifested in the higher incidence of poverty and landlessness. Smallholders are marginalised and transformed into landless people (Shrestha 1997). This means that a few landlords control a huge fraction of the country's land. The Nepalese land resource is besieged by multifarious problems such as duel ownership in land tenure, fragmentation, unequal distribution, institutional obstacles and unfocused government policies. Dual ownership is severely limiting productivity because neither owner nor tenants invest in the land.[4]

Legal measures to implement land reform, to prevent land fragmentation, and to promote land consolidation are ineffective (Ghimire 1992; New Era 1988). Because of a lack of effective land-use planning, the agricultural sector is not able to reach its potential through specialisation and diversification. Erosion, landslides and floods in the Hill areas have seriously affected the river banks, the lower slopes of the Hills and the fertile land of the Terai region, and have had a negative impact on agriculture, irrigation, hydro-electricity, forest, bio-diversity, the environment, road systems, transport and tourism.

Land management practices in Nepal are still insensitive to the negative effects on the wider environment, and become a source of conflict. For example, cultivation on the steep-slope land in the foothills of the Himalayas in Nepal is contributing to floods in the delta areas of Bangladesh (Tear Fund 1999). Buildings are rapidly covering highly fertile lands of the Terai region and urban centres as city centres expand. The land reform campaign, although initiated in 1951, has so far been merely a political slogan rather than significantly contributing to its reform. All major political parties have highlighted the land reform agenda in their election manifestos, but none of them are fulfilling their commitments.

Despite the fact that the government, donors and local communities are investing much more effort, time and money in natural resource management, and despite the fact that several natural resource related offices have been established in all districts, environmental scarcity and conflicts are growing (Upreti 2004). My previous research findings show that conflicts are increasing through the intervention of external development organisations without a proper understanding of local systems, lack of user participation in natural resource management and defective policies (Upreti 2000a, b, c, 2002). Therefore it is time to rethink the dominant natural resource management approach in Nepal. Evidence is accumulating that, despite the efforts of the government, donors and NGOs, environmental problems and resource scarcity are mounting and leading to conflict and violence.

Perhaps nobody would disagree that bad environmental governance has created

---

[4] The Rural Credit Survey of Nepal Rastra Bank (1994) has indicated that investment in land improvement in Nepal is less than 3% of household income.

resources scarcity leading to conflict. Resource degradation, conflict about access, rights and obligations, fair distribution, maintenance and benefit sharing were basically under-emphasised in governance practices in Nepal. Various endogenous and exogenous factors such as population growth, globalisation of markets, and environmental and technological changes are imposing new conflict on the natural resources sector. Many large and small natural resource management projects implemented by different agencies are introducing new conflicts as well as having various negative impacts on society. For example, ignorance of the importance of indigenous knowledge in planning and designing new systems, extortion, alteration of local rights and regulations, the replacement of old institutions by new ones, and the imposition of technocratic solutions are some of the immediate implications of the new interventions. These interventions have their own firmly fixed and uniform policy and a rigid procedure based on reductionist-positivist orientation. They are technocratic in nature and generally do not acknowledge local diversities. This is becoming one of the major causes of conflict in natural resource management.

Conflict arises if the new natural resource management policy of the government conflicts with local cultural practice. The economic motive of people to acquire more from the existing natural resources on a competitive basis also leads to conflict. Conflict is also growing as a result of the contradiction between environmental and economic interests. Changes in historical use patterns of natural resource use can bring conflict into a community. Similarly, contradictions between legal arrangements and customary practices have promoted several conflicts.

The social dimension of natural resource management is crucial in natural resource-related conflicts. The social dimension refers to the more human-related aspects of negotiations, such as knowledge, institutions of technology, and forums (platforms) (Röling 2000). In the study of conflict it is important to understand the role of the human dimension in respect of natural resources (Röling 1997). In the contemporary development discourse natural resources are usually perceived as hard,[5] objectively fixed, bio-physical facts (e.g., soil, crops, livestock, disease and

---

[5] Röling (1997) illustrates the notion of soft and hard science in natural resource management in his commonly used term "Soft Side of Land Perspective'. It is important to look beyond the common categorisation of social science as soft science and technical science (biophysical) as hard science. It implies that positivist and constructivist thinking exists within both sciences. For example, even within

pests, water, yields, erosion, caring capacity, bio-diversity, physical properties) Such factors as human goals, organisation and technological aspects (Röling 2000) are usually ignored. But conflict concerning natural resources is the outcome of societal arrangement, human intention and behaviour (Röling 1997) framed within those biophysical properties. Therefore, both of these dimensions of natural resources are essential for a better understanding of conflicts in natural resource management. Resource management decisions and the activities of resource users, the performance of bureaucracy, the functioning of user groups and associations, access to and control over resources, customary practices and state laws/regulations, livelihood requirements and the welfare of people are therefore important issues to be addressed in any study of conflict.

In Nepal the dominant development paradigm still treats technology as a 'black box' and gives little attention to human intentions and behaviour in managing natural resources. Responsive institutions, collective learning, negotiation and concerted actions in my opinion are vital but neglected components in natural resource management discourses and practices. Several researchers and academics (for example, Röling 1997; Pradhan *et al.* 2000; Uphoff 2000, Chambers 1988) have shown that natural resource management is not only a technical domain, but that it is more importantly a social discourse, shaped and influenced by social processes and intentional human activities. A plural legal situation can create several conflicts because of its uncertain and manipulative nature. Most of the legal reforms related to natural resources have yet to be translated into real practices. If and when they are practised, power brokers manipulate them and the weaker section of society still feels uncertain and insecure.

During my twenty-five years of practical experience in the rural development, natural resource management and environmental sectors, I have increasingly realised that a government's policies and a donor's strategies are more focused on management and control of natural resources through prescriptive technical solutions than through a meaningful participation of people. This leads to conflict and disturbance in the self-regulated use of ecological systems. We are now entering the twenty-first century, where conflict between economic objectives and

---

the social sciences there are both positivist thinking, such as the resolution of conflict by enforcing acts and regulations and use of the courts and police, and constructivist thinking such as the resolution of conflict through learning, negotiation and collaboration.

sustainable ecological use of natural resources is accelerating. Obviously the increasing problems such as the lack of pure drinking water, loss of bio-diversity, climate change, environment pollution and other ecological challenges are the product of increasingly developed consumerism, population pressure, economic motives and governance failure. These problems are not only disrupting self-sustaining NR systems but also creating severe conflicts in society. Therefore, an economically guided focus for these problems is in itself a source of further conflict.

### 3.1 Case one: mis-governance in a donor-funded irrigation system

In 1982 a local leader requested the Department of Irrigation (DOI) to construct an irrigation canal. The DOI conducted a survey but did not proceed any further. This project came into the light again when a District Irrigation Office (DIO) was established in Dolakha district in 1989. An active local political worker (hereinafter referred as the initiator), who was also a professional contractor, by using his 'relation of special intimacy'[6] (Wade 1982) with engineers initiated this project. The DIO Engineer approved the project within the provisions of the Asian Development Bank (ADB) funded Irrigation Sector Support Project (ISSP).

Difficulties started when the local people discovered that the proposed alignment of the canal had been changed.[7] A Water Users Committee (WUC) was formed without informing villagers and they elected chairmen of the two Village Development Committees (VDCs) of the command area of the canal. So the conflict became more serious and the public started to oppose the activities of the WUC. Users of the canals downstream raised the issue of water scarcity. As a consequence, the disgruntled people lodged a complaint to the District Administration Office to stop the construction. The Chief District Officer organised meetings with both groups and an agreement was reached with the following provisions:

(a)     sharing of water with downstream canals,

---

[6] Bargaining for a bribe between contractor and engineer is more direct and surreptitious in the developed relation of special intimacy (Wade 1982).

[7] According to the respondents the motive for the change of alignment of the canal was to increase the total cost of the project.

(b)     sharing of power by reorganising the existing WUC of the project, and

(c)     sharing of construction work and budget by users.

Accordingly, the existing 11-member WUC was expanded to 19 members. The newly expanded WUC divided the total construction work into 35 sections and allocated these to WUC members and their supporters. However, 85% of the people that obtained construction contracts were not beneficiaries of the project. Therefore they were not much interested in constructing a canal of good quality, and did not use the proper ratio of cement to concrete, nor quality construction materials, seeking to save money on the ground. Most of the people who got contracts were either WUC members themselves or their close relatives and supporters.

The technology used in the project was expensive and complicated. The irrigation technicians, in consultation with the WUC used cemented structures, masonry, gabion wire etc. to raise the cost of the project, as this gave ample scope to get commissions while purchasing, and they could save a huge amount out of the transportation cost of the construction materials. The quality of work was poor because they were not using construction materials according to the standard norm, in order to save money (Upreti 2001), doing what Wade (1982) describes as 'saving in the ground' and Thapa (2002) and Panday (2001) describe as 'corruption'. In this way, full of conflicts and tension the project was officially completed in 1996. Today only the canal track remains and the WUC is completely dysfunctional. The villagers filed a case for corruption against the WUC in 1995. This was dismissed by a Special Police Investigation in the same year. Local people blamed that the alleged offer by the WUC of a bribe to dismiss the case (Upreti 2001). This type of manipulation and corruption is not new in the development programme in Nepal (Panday 2001; Thapa 2002). In this context, Hari Bahadur Thapa has made a thorough analysis of Nepalese corruption in his recent book entitled *Anatomy of Corruption*. He writes:

> Corruption has flourished because of lack of strong political will to control it. Nepal's political leadership has been more concerned with its own party political interests than the welfare of the nation (Thapa 2002: iv).

*3.2 Case two: conflict between the farmers of an irrigation system*

A deep conflict was observed over an irrigation system when the government expanded the existing canal in Pawoti village of Dolakha District. In consequence of this work the existing rules and regulations were replaced, water scarcity was observed and tension between different farmers and between the farmers and the irrigation authority mounted. Before the external intervention irrigation conflicts had been resolved by users themselves using locally developed rules and procedures. Water sharing and maintenance of the canal was effective. Afterwards people were unhappy with the misuse of money received from the government and stopped contributing their volunteer labour to maintain the canal. The conflict became very serious and generally tail-end farmers were not allowed to take water. These farmers approached the local authority, district irrigation offices, and the district administration but the conflict was not resolved because the government authority was not willing to solve the problem. Instead, the conflict became increasingly politicised, the canal became dysfunctional and the villagers fell in to deep conflict. The main causes of this conflict were ignorance of the rules developed and enforced by the community, and of the voice of local people, and the ineffective role of the government organisations responsible for addressing conflict.

*3.3 Case three: conflict between the village elite and the local people in a pastureland*

Access and control of the pastureland located in Ward 7 of the Pawoti VDC was the main cause of this conflict. Local elite and powerbrokers started to terrace the centuries-old communally managed public pastureland. Being powerful politicians of high economic status and with strong network connections with bureaucrats, the pastureland invaders seriously undermined the symbolic and economic attachment of the local community to this land. When the users started to protest against the invasion the conflict escalated. Local efforts over several years failed to resolve the conflict. Ultimately, the case reached the senior government administrator. The administrator decided in favour of the community but the invaders did not leave the invaded land. The community members appealed for the execution of the earlier decision, but the power and influence of the powerbrokers prevented an effective enforcement of the decision and the appeal was dismissed. The legal procedure was too complicated and expensive for the community. Therefore, they did not go for further legal remedies. The conflict continues and the society is divided.

### 3.4 Case four: conflict between two communities over a spring water source

A serious conflict between two communities over the sharing of water from a spring was observed in Pawoti VDC. The existing water users were not prepared to share this water source. They claimed that there would be a problem of scarcity of water to irrigate their fields if they shared the source with another community. The case went to the government's district office but was not settled. It was politicised by the district politicians influencing the government bureaucrats. So the conflict remained unsettled for several years. Later, with the help of a local priest, a women's leader and a local NGO, the conflict was resolved with the following provisions:

1.  the new users should construct a reservoir tank close to the source and collect water at night time;
2.  in case of water shortage during rice transplanting, water should not be collected in the reservoir tank during that time;
3.  the new users should take responsibility for the conservation of the source;
4.  the existing users should inform the new users before letting the water flow out for rice transplanting;
5.  both groups should apologise for past accusations and misunderstandings; and
6.  if problems emerged, the users would have to call a meeting to find ways to resolve them.

This proposal was thoroughly discussed in successive meetings with the existing users, staff of the NGO, other villagers and the new users. They used their past experiences, learnt from their mistakes, and worked collectively to settle the conflict. In this way the serious conflict, which could not be solved by the government agency, was solved at local level with win-win outcome.

### 3.5 Case five: conflict between the landlords and the tenants in agricultural lands

A deep-seated conflict between the 123 tenant households and 50 landlords of the

Deurali village of the Pawoti VDC was resolved after 39 years through several efforts at different levels. The landlords had been a rich and powerful ruling elite in the village for several generations. So they were not ready to accept the demands for tenants' rights from their tenants. The tenant farmers made all possible local efforts to establish their rights over the land. They mobilised local priests, relatives of landlords, and themselves approached the landowners to engage in negotiation, but these efforts did not work. They also paid the price of the land to the landowners to induce them to transfer the land. But the landlords did not transfer the land ownership. Because of the complicated nature of the legal procedure, high fees and the potential fear that the decision would go against them because of the influence of power and money, the tenants did not opt for a legal battle. Instead they stopped paying the rent. Then the landlords filed a case against them. The governmental organisations responsible for dealing with land conflicts gave a verdict in favour of the landlords. The tenants did not accept the decision and continued with their claim. The tenants were strongly organised, learnt from past mistakes while dealing with landowners, discussed their problems with other people in the village, and won the support of all villagers. The determination and concerted actions of the tenants forced the landowners to rethink the issue. The landlords realised that the solution of evicting them from the land would not work. If the tenants were evicted they would be landless and create severe problems and even pose a risk of physical insecurity to the landlords. Finally the landowners transferred the ownership rights to the tenants and the tenants paid 100,000 rupees in return. Then the conflict was resolved locally in a win-win situation.

## 4. A Framework for Resource Governance and its Legal Dimensions

I define resource governance as a set of policies, laws and regulations, institutions, technologies and cognitive aspects like values, perceptions, understanding and actions, through which people manage (conserve and utilise) natural resources in a transparent, accountable, participatory and equitable manner. Generally resource governance covers:

- setting broad objectives,
- planning for specific targets, and framing policies to attain those targets,
- selecting specific policy instruments,
- establishing institutional mechanisms to implement them, and

- adopting appropriate approaches for involvement and
  empowerment of stakeholders.

All these elements give rise to conflict if not handled properly. This dimension is
discussed in detail in this section. Conflicts in Nepal over lands, water and forests
are given an analysis in this section based on the concept of resource governance
systems.

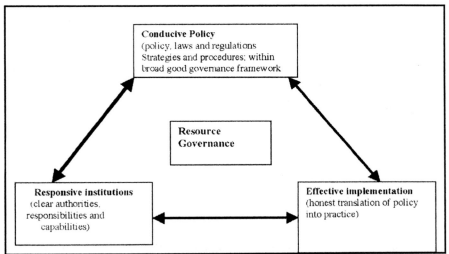

Fig. Interrelationship between diff components of environmental governance

Figure 1.  Interrelationship between components of environmental governance

Though weak in their implementation, several international efforts have been made
in environmental governance. Nepal is a signatory of more than 22 Multilateral
Environmental Agreements (MEAs) (Silwal and Prasad 2002) and works within
international guiding principles and frameworks.

His Majesty's Government of Nepal uses general policy documents like Periodic
Five Year Plans, the National Conservation Strategy (NCS) 1988, the EIA
Guidelines 1993/1997, the Nepal Environmental Policy and Action Plan (NEPAP I
1995 and II 1996), the Sustainable Development Agenda of Nepal (SDAN) 2002,
and sectoral policy documents like the Agriculture Perspective Plan (APP), the
Hydropower Development Policy 1992/2002, the Forestry Policy 1992, the
Industrial Policy 1992, Nepal Environmental Health Initiatives (NEHI) 1997, and

the Cleaner Production Policy 2001 (Silwal and Prasad 2002) to facilitate environmental governance practice.

In Part 4, Article 26 (State Policies) of the Constitution of the Kingdom of Nepal, 1990 stipulates:

> (3) The State shall pursue a policy of mobilizing the natural resources and heritage of the country in manner, which might be useful and beneficial to the interest of the nation;
> (4) The State shall give priority to the protection of the environment and also to the prevention of its further damage due to physical development activities by increasing the awareness of the general public about environmental cleanliness, and the State shall also make arrangements for the special protection of the rare wildlife, the forest and the vegetation.

To meet the constitutional requirement there are two specific enactments, i.e., the Environmental Protection Act (EPA) 1997 and the Environmental Protection Regulations (EPR) 1998. These two provisions govern access to environmental services. In addition to that there are other acts supporting environmental governance (Box 2).

In addition to these provisions there are also some other important provisions such as the Parliamentary Council for Conservation of Natural & Cultural Resources (CCNCR), the Environment Conservation Council, the Parliament, National Planning Commission (NPC), Environment Protection Council (EPC), Water and Energy Commission (WEC), etc. (Silwal and Prasad, 2002).

| Box 2 | |
|---|---|
| Acts and Laws | |
| **Agriculture related**: Pesticide Act 1992/Rules 1994; Livestock Health and Service Act, 1998 /Rules 1999; Seed Act, 1989/ Rules, 1996; Food Act, 1967; Aquatic Animals Protection Act, 1961. | **Land related**: Land Act, 1964; Land (Measurement) Act, 1963; Land Revenue Act, 1979; Land and Watershed Protection Act, 1983; Soil and Water Conservation Act, 1992. |
| **Air related**: Vehicular and Transport Management Act, 1992. | **Water related:** Water Resources Act, 1992; Electricity Act, 1992. |
| **Forest related**: Forest Act, 1993. | **Industry related**: Industrial Management Act, 1992; Industrial Enterprise Act, 1992; Labor Act, 1991. |

**Local Self Governance Act (LSGA), 1999.** The LSGA provides more autonomy to Village Development Committees (VDCs), District Development Committees (DDCs) and Municipalities by empowering the local authorities to manage natural resources, and guides them to integrate environmental resources and environmental planning (Part V, 5.3). Some of the highlights that pertain to environmental governance are:

wards are required to help in the protection of the environment through plantations (Section 25[e]);
rights and duties of the VDCs are stipulated (Section 28)
VDCs are empowered to levy taxes on utilization of natural resources (Section 55);
property of VDCs, i.e. natural resources, are listed (Section 68)
powers are provided to formulate and implement plans for the conservation of forest, vegetation, biological diversity and soil (Section 189);
power is given to formulate bylaws in the area of management of all the natural resources i.e. air, water, land and forest.

Source: Silwal and Prasad 2002.

## 5. Political Economy of Natural Resources in Nepal

Political economy refers to the public power or decision-making over access to and control over resources. The basic questions are, who gains, who loses, who has control, and how? In discussing the political economy of natural resources it is important to examine how politics function in a particular social setting. In the agrarian society of Nepal people use the land, but the true owner is the state and a feudalistic mode of production exists. Society is not a mere sum of individual acts, but rather a complex totality of interacting individuals tied up with specific social and economic relationships and interdependent structures. Individuals in society are embedded in particular class relationships and class interests. Political life is an expression of dependency and state domination. The elite, particularly the formal power holders, have an interest in maintaining such a dependent structure so as to gain the most advantage from the system for themselves. This is truly reflected in Nepalese rural societies where there are hierarchies of chains of relationships, which have an exploitative structure. There is a formal power structure that is represented by the elite at different levels. At the political level there are the top civil servants, businessmen, religious leaders, etc. At the local level these elites advance their interests through power. They share certain common ideologies and political positions, values and perspectives and act accordingly to maintain the existing mode of resource management and utilisation. Investment of resources in development is organised accordingly.

The history of the Nepalese political economy of natural resources shows that prior to 1734, when the present-day Nepal was a fragmented groups of petty states, people were deliberately encouraged to cultivate as much forest and pasture land as possible. This ensured them a good living and increased the productivity of the land. They then paid a certain portion of their returns to the state (Regmi 1978). Until 1950 it was common for the state to grant tax-free land to officials, religious organisations and individual favourites of the kings or rulers. Traditionally land was considered as the property of the state [state landlordism] and this land is called *Raikar*[8]. Only the state had the right to alienate land through sale, mortgage

---

[8] M.C. Regmi argues that there were mainly two types of land tenure system in Nepal, i.e., *Raikar* and *Kipat*. All other tenured forms of land were derived from *Raikar* (Regmi 1976, 1978). The meaning of *Raikar* land has changed since 1951, from crown land to land owned by individuals. *Raikar*-land ownership denotes an

or bequest (Regmi 1976). Using this right of alienation the state granted cultivated or uncultivated state-owned *Raikar* lands to individuals in the form of *Jagir, Birta, Rakam, Sera and Rajya*, and charitable or religious organisations in the form of *Guthi* (Regmi 1976). [9] The *Guthi* land tenure system also included the endowment of private lands (obtained from the state) by individual landlords for religious

---

ultimate state ownership over those lands, which were actually cultivated by individuals as direct tenants of the state. The tenancy of *Rraikar* land has two categories, the actual tenant-cultivators and the tenant owners. The latter category of tenants are those who pay rent to the state, but who can sell or bequeath their *Raikar* land, whereas the former category (the tenant cultivators) have no right to sell sublet or otherwise alienate the land which has been allotted to them. The usufructuary assignment of *Raikar* land to individuals and institutions is a deliberate means of rewarding them and ensuring their loyalty, paying them for services rendered and promoting social and religious activities. The *Raikar* land grant was practised in several forms viz.: *Birta, Jagir* and *Guthi, Rakam, Rajya, and Sera*.

[9] A *Birta* grant was given to a noble as a reward for a service rendered to the state. It had no time limits and it could be rented out or inherited until confiscated or recalled by the state. *Birta* owners usually had full rights to possess, occupy, sell, lease, subdivide and bequeath their lands. Most *Birta* lands were not taxable. They have become the foundation of the modern, private landed property arrangement. *Jagir* land holding was more conditional and subtle and often granted to government servants rather than to members of the ruling elite. A *Jagir* assessment was usually an assignment of the income from *Raikar* lands in lieu of a salary and it could not be assigned or sold. *Jagir* rights lapsed on the cesser of employment, or at the discretion of the government. The *Birta* and *Jagir* forms were abolished in 1959, with the enactment of the *Birta* Abolition Act and were converted to *Raikar* land (New Era 1988: 28-31). *Sera* was a form of land tenure explicitly used by the royal palace to meet the food-grain and other land-related requirements. *Rakam* is another form of land tenure where cultivators have to compulsorily provide unpaid labourers to the government as carpenters, masons, and postmen. *Rajya* was another modified form of land tenure granted as the princely state award for members and relatives of Royal families. This land-granting practice was common, up until the *Rana* regime. Rulers granted large portion of lands to soldiers as Jagir to keep them under their control. *Rana* rulers confined the land-grant practices to their relatives and key officials.

purposes. *Kipat*[10] was another communal land-tenure system whereby individuals derived land rights from their association with particular ethnic groups, located in a particular area. Regmi states that "individuals who cultivated land in their capacity as a member of a *Kipat*-owing ethnic group owed allegiance primarily to the community, not to the state" (Regmi 1972: 27).

Almost one-third of agricultural and forest land of the nation was granted to private individuals by 1950 and the remainder belongs to *Rana* (members of the ruling clan) themselves (Regmi 1978). Local functionaries, all favourites of *Rana*, implemented the land-grant policy in the villages and were able to assure most benefit for themselves. They obtained a great deal of land from the state through *Jagir* and *Birta* grants and rented these lands to peasant farmers under tenancy arrangements. In this way local functionaries turned into landlords. Peasant farmers had to pay half of their crop yield as rent to the local landlords. Gradually, to ensure their rent, landlords introduced the *kut* (contract) system where only those tenants who were able to pay high rents could get a contract. Irrespective of the performance of their crops, even if the crops failed, farmers had to pay rent as *Kut*. Eventually these peasant farmers effectively turned into slave labourers of the *Jagir* and *Birta* holders (Regmi 1978). After 1951 the government nationalised all the forest in Nepal so as to release land from the grip of *Birta* holders, especially from *Rana* families. However, this did not function well in practice. Historically land resources in Nepal played a crucial role in socio-economic and political change and were used by principalities and national governments for their political goals.

Large portions of all these forms of land tenure were cultivated under tenancy arrangements, in the form of sharecropping. Some landlords were entrusted by the government as *Mukhiya* in the Hill regions and *Chaudhari* and *Jimidar* in Terai regions to work on land administration (Pradhan *et al.* 2000). They had the authority to establish settlements in new areas, and to collect tax and pay part of it to government (Regmi 1976). The emergence of a unified nation was the outcome of the consolidation of small kingdoms, fiefdoms and principalities. The state began to regulate the available natural resources to generate government revenue.

---

[10] This was an ancient type of communal land tenure where an ethnic community was granted land by their king in recognition of a traditional communal tenure. Headmen had the authority to grant individuals the right to cultivate certain areas and to collect forest products from other areas (Regmi 1978)

This led to the establishment of control mechanisms: different departments and regional offices, policies, acts, rules and regulations to control systematically the available natural resources. It can be seen from the above brief history of land tenure systems in Nepal that the rulers used land as a means of maintaining functionaries for the consolidation of power and maintaining good relations with family members, close allies, members of the nobility, military personnel, civil employees, royal courtiers and potential foes. The mode of production in and distribution of natural resources was very much feudalistic in nature.

In the history of Nepalese development (especially between 1951 and 2000), development intervention as a means of agrarian change has had three complementary objectives: (i) to raise production and productivity, (ii) to raise livelihood,[11] and (iii) to sustain the existing natural resource base. The emphasis given in national policies and planning (in, for example, the Ninth Five Year Plan (NFYP), and the Nepal Agriculture Perspective Plan (APP)) was to increase production, achieve a trade balance and increase employment opportunities in the natural resource sector; and enhance national economic growth by effectively utilising the available natural resources. However, the performance level of such intervention in alleviating poverty in Nepal has not yet reached expectations. There is evidence that productivity-oriented achievements are not fully able to address problems such as the widening gap between rich and poor, unemployment, and degradation of the natural resource base. These problems are not only creating inequality but are also creating fundamental conflict between the rich and the poor. The growing Maoist movement in Nepal is an example of such conflict. The implications of such conflicts are long term and are dividing society, and disrupting social harmony and cohesion. In this context Chambers explains that "the problem of poverty in South Asia at least is not now a problem of production, or of food availability: it is a problem of who produces the food and of who has power to obtain it" (Chambers 1988:7).

---

[11] Chambers (1988) explained the first and second objectives in detail in the context of South Asia. According to him livelihood thinking "is assessed in terms of the adequate and secured livelihoods it generates and sustains, putting antipoverty efforts, and people, before production *per se*"( Chambers 1988: 7).

---

Box 3

Impacts of Development Intervention in Conflict

Mohan Mainali has severely questioned the contribution and effectiveness of donor funded development intervention to address the root causes of the conflict. He writes:

> ... What we say of the USAID implemented Rapti Zone Rural Area Dec Project, and its second incarnation, the Rapti Development Project, aimed to fulfil the basic needs of the poor majority, the farmers of the mid hills. The Programme spent about US$ 50m in "improving household food production and consumption, improving income generating opportunities for poor farmers, landless labourers, occupational castes and women". In short, the project's overall goal was to increase the well-being of people. The Americans thought they'd need 15 years to achieve their objectives. And, going by their reports, they worked 'hard' for those 15 years. The project started in 1980 and ended in 1995, just a month and a half before the Maoists began their armed movement.... The government and donors both say development packages will help eliminate the Maoists. If that were true, why was Rapti Zone so favourable for the development of Maoist movement? If that is what you get after 15 years of American funded development, we were perhaps better without it. (Mainali 2003: 125-126)

## 6. The Denial Psyche in Nepalese Conflict:

The denial psyche is a unique characteristic of Nepalese society. Nobody is ready to acknowledge their own weaknesses in addressing the current conflict. Parliamentary parties are not ready to accept their failure as one of the main causes of the conflict. The government is not ready to accept the fact did not take correct approach to address this conflict; the rebels are not ready to accept that the general public want peace and not the violence. They are all denying that all of them are equally responsible for the escalation of this conflict. Bureaucracy denies its failure, the NGO sector denies its malpractices in the name of development. The business community denies the very fact that businessmen are among the top promoters of corruption in this country. The donor community denies their failure to support development in this country. Professionals deny their professional failure. So all major actors deny the reality and their own weakness and put the blame on others and shift the responsibilities onto others.

---

Box 4

### Paradox of Conflict

Paradoxically empowerment led to conflict in Nepal. A plausible explanation of the emergence of the Maoist conflict in a particular time is the growing awareness and empowerment of the Nepalese people during the initial years of multiparty democracy. People have become more aware of poverty, inequality, discrimination, corruption and lack of employment opportunities. They are empowered to raise their voices against injustice, poverty and social exclusion. Therefore, paradoxically the current crisis is not only the syndrome of system failure but also an indicator of social awareness and people's empowerment. Multiparty democracy gave ample opportunities for different categories of people to organise, to form organisations to fight for their rights, and these helped tremendously to empower people.

---

The individual and collective political psyche has so far preferred to ignore reality rather than to face challenges that are threatening Nepali democracy. A powerful defence mechanism, used by politicians and power centres alike, is denial. They deny the seriousness of the current situation, afraid to admit that their prevailing attitudes and practices are inappropriate and causing problems. They feel even more obstinately defensive when Nepali people confront them with evidence that their actions need to change. In Nepal denial is rooted in the individual and institutional level in politics, in political parties, in government departments, and in other power centres. The difficulty of overcoming this magnitude of denial by democratic reform should not be underestimated. It is necessary to replace the ideas, values, greed and orthodoxy that underlie formidable and complex obstacles with a new set of ideas and values. If this paradigm shift is accepted as inevitable, the current conflict may be a great opportunity for fundamental reform of Nepali society.

---

Box 5

### The Nepalese Crisis is a Complex Mix of Everything

Acute inequalities, absolute poverty, lack of access to resources and the failure of political structures to address these issues, have made Nepali society extremely vulnerable to conflict and mass movements like the Maoists' 'people's war'. Several examples from Peru, Chile, Mozambique, India, Nicaragua, Tanzania, Senegal and Columbia show that resistance from below is obvious and predictable if the state is not responsive to basic concerns of the rural poor. Deep rooted social cleavages in terms of caste, ethnicity, gender and regional, cultural, linguistic and religious forms of discrimination provided fertile ground for conflict to escalate. The Maoists successfully capitalised on the highly unsatisfactory democratic transition of 1990. The people of Nepal are deeply disillusioned by the poor performance of current political structures and processes. The dominance of certain groups in all social, political and economic sectors has bred strong feelings of injustice and revenge, as the socially marginalised people strongly believe that they have been excluded from opportunities and resources. The Maoists have tactically exploited this resentment. The emergence of ethnic interest groups, and increased awareness of social exclusion and ethnic inequalities and governance failure further fuelled the conflict.

## 7. Conclusion

The raising of productivity[12] still dominates thinking in Nepal. Environmental governance is not getting the required attention in the broader national governance system. Resource use and environmental services are taken for granted. The severe implications of resource scarcity and disruption of fundamental ecological processes are either not internalised or deliberately ignored in a realm of growing consumerism and the economically driven profit-making motive. Natural resources

---

[12] Both the Ninth Five-Year Plan and the Agriculture Perspective Plan focused exclusively on economic growth of the agricultural sector through effective natural resource management.

have strong and diverse impacts on different categories of people such as landless farmers, wage labourers, tenant farmers, women, landlords and powerful elites. The sustainable contribution of natural resource management in reducing the vulnerability of impoverished people, sustaining ecological services from natural resources, stabilising social mobility and improving the quality of life of the rural poor is yet to materialise. Conflict mitigation and the addressing of environmental scarcity are beyond the dominant development paradigm. Sustainable use and management of natural resources can only take place through a strong political commitment, clear vision, fair and responsive administration, protection from malpractice such as rent-seeking (Wade 1982), expansion of institutional understanding (Ostrom 1990), and the embrace of collective learning and concerted action (Röling and Wagemakers 1998). These crucial elements of environmental governance are severely lacking at present. The economic transformation of the more than 49%of Nepalese people who are below the poverty line is still more wishful thinking than a reality. In contemporary Nepal ethics and responsibility (providing basic livelihoods to the burgeoning population) do not drive natural resource management objectives, but rather they are driven by the drive towards the accumulation of wealth and power.

# References

BECK, Ulrich, Anthony GIDDENS and S. LAS (eds.)
1994    *Reflective Modernisation: Politics Tradition and Aesthetics in Modern Social Order*. Cambridge: Polity Press.
BUCKLES, D. (ed.)
1999    *Cultivating Peace: Conflict and Collaboration in Natural Resource Management*. Ottawa/Washington: IDRC/ World Bank Institute.
CBS (Central Bureau of Statistics)
1995    *Statistical Year Book of Nepal 1995*. Kathmandu: Central Bureau of Statistics.
CHAMBERS R.
1988    *Managing Canal Irrigation: Practical Analysis from South Asia*. New Delhi: Oxford University Press.
DANIELS, Steven E. and Gregg B. WALKER
1997    'Rethinking public participation in natural resource management: concepts from pluralism and five emerging approaches.' Pp. 29-48 in *Pluralism and Sustainable Forestry and Rural Development*, Proceedings of an

International Workshop, 9-12 December, 1997. Rome: FAO.

ENGEL, P.G.H. and S.M.L. SALOMON (eds.)

1997    *Facilitating Innovation for Development: A RAAKS Resource Guide.* Amsterdam: KIT Press.

GHIMIRE, K.

1992    *Forest or Farm? The Politics of Poverty and Land Hunger in Nepal.* Delhi: Oxford University Press.

HMG/N (His Majesty's Government of Nepal)

1992    *National Report on United Nations Conference on Environment and Development.* Kathmandu: His Majesty's Government of Nepal.

IDRIS S.M.M.

1998    *Why? Why? Why...? Half of the Sky: The Struggle of the Women in the Third World.* Malaysia: The Third World Resource. No 94. 1998.

JHPIP (Johns Hopkins Population Information Programme)

1998    *World Report of Johns Hopkins Population Information Programme.* Baltimore: Johns Hopkins Population Information Programme.

LUBCHENCO J.

1998    'Entering the century of environment: A new social contract for science.' *Science* 279: 491-496.

MAINALI M,

2003    'Development vs the Maobadies.' Pp. 125-127 in: D. Thapa (ed.), *Understanding the Maoist Movement in Nepal.* Kathmandu: Martin Chautari.

NEW ERA

1988    *A Study of Legal System and Legal Situation in Rural Areas of the Kingdom of Nepal.* Kathmandu: Friedirich Naumann Foundation.

NPC (National Planning Commission)

1998    *Ninth Plan 1997-2002.* Kathmandu: National Planning Commission.

OHLSSON L. (ed.)

1995    *Hydropolitics: Conflict over Water as Development Constraints.* London and New Jersey: ZED Books.

OLI, K.P.

1998    *Conflict Resolution and Mediation in Natural Resource Management.* Kathmandu: IUCN-Nepal.

OSTROM E.

1990    *Governing the Commons: The Evolution of Institutions for Collective Actions.* New York: Cambridge University Press.

PANDAY, D.R.

2001    *Corruption, governance and international co-operation: essays and impressions on Nepal and South Asia.* Kathmandu: Transparency International Nepal.

PRADHAN, R., F. von BENDA-BECKMANN and K. von BENDA-BECKMANN (eds.)

2000    *Water Land and Laws: Changing Rights to Land and Water in Nepal.* Kathmandu: FREEDEAL.

REGMI, M.C.

1972    *A Study of Nepali Economic History 1768-1846.* Delhi: Adroit Publishers.

1976    *Land Ownership in Nepal.* Berkeley: University of California Press.

1978    *Land Tenure and Taxation in Nepal.* Kathmandu: Ratna Pustak Bhandar.

RÖLING, N.

1997    'The soft side of land.' *ITC Journal* 3 and 4, Special Congress Issue: 248-262.

2000    *Gateway to the Global Garden: Beta/Gamma Science for Dealing with Ecological Rationality.* Eighth Annual Hopper Lecture October 24, 2000. University of Guelph, Canada.

RÖLING, N. and A. WAGEMAKERS (eds.)

1998    *Facilitating Sustainable Agriculture.* Cambridge: Cambridge University Press.

SHRESTHA, N.R.

1997    *In the Name of Development: A Reflection in Nepal.* Kathmandu: Educational Enterprise.

SILWAL, P.K. and H. PRASAD

2002    *Environmental Governance: AQ Manual for Local Authorities in Nepal.* Kathmandu: UNDP.

TEAR FUND

1999    'Looking after our land.' *Footsteps* 41 (Dec.) Teddington: Tear Fund.

THAPA, H.B.

2002    *Anatomy of Corruption.* Kathmandu: Published by Sangita Thapa.

UPHOFF, N.

2000    'Understanding social capital: learning from the analysis and experience of Participation. HLR: http://www.sls.wau.nl/mi/Education/index.html, circulated for a group presentation on Wednesday 13 September 2000, Wageningen.

UPRETI, B.R.

1999    'Managing local conflicts over water resources: A case study from Nepal.' *AgREN, ODI Network Paper* No 95, July. London: Overseas Development Institute.

2000a   'Beyond rhetorical success: advancing the potential for the Nepalese community forestry programme to address equity concerns.' In: E. Wollenberg, D. Edmunds, L. Buck, J. Fox and S. Brodt (eds.), *Social Learning in Community Forest Management: Linking Concept and Practice,* a Joint Publication of CIFOR and the East-West Centre.

2000b 'Community level water use negotiation practice: an implication for water resource management.' Pp. 249-269 in: R. Pradhan, F. von Benda-Beckmann and K. von Benda-Beckmann (eds.).

2000c The effects of changing land use systems in agricultural biodiversity: experiences and lessons from Nepal.' Pp. 327-337 in: Xu Jianchu (Ed.) *Links Between the Culture and Biodiversity,* Proceedings of the Culture and Biodiversity Congress, 20-30 July, Cunming, Yunnan, China, 21-30 July 2000. Yunnan Science and Technology.

2001 *Conflict Management in Natural Resources: A Study of Land, Water and Forest Conflict in Nepal.* Published PhD Dissertation. Wagenignen University.

2002 *Management of Social and Natural Resource Conflict in Nepal: Reality and Alternative.* Adroit Publishers, New Delhi.

2003 'Environmental governance to address resource scarcity and conflict in Nepal.' Paper presented at *Environmental Conflict Resolution: A Right Based Approach,* organised by Environmental Law Committee of Nepal Bar Association, Kathmandu, 7th June.

2004 *The price of Neglect: Resources Conflict to Maoist Insurgency in the Himalayan Kingdom.* Kathmandu: Bhrikuti Publishers.

WADE R.
1982 'The study of administrative and political corruption: canal irrigation in south India.' *Journal of Development Studies* 18: 287-328.

WALKER G.B. and S.E. DANIELS
1997 'Foundations of natural resource conflict: conflict theory and public policy. Pp. 13-36 in: B. Solberg and S. Miina (eds.), *Conflict Management and Public Participation in Land Management,* EFT Proceeding No 14. European Forest Institute.

WARNER, M. and P. JONES
1998 'Assessing the need to manage conflict in community based natural resource project.' *Natural Resource Perspective* 35 (Aug.) London: Overseas Development Institute.

WORLD WATER FORUM
2000 *A Vision of Water for Food and Rural Development.* The Hague: World Water Council.

# THEORIZING FORMAL PLURALISM: QUANTIFICATION OF LEGAL PLURALISM FOR SPATIO – TEMPORAL ANALYSIS

Yüksel Sezgin

## Introduction

Israel is a legally pluralistic society. So is India. And they both have been legally pluralistic societies throughout their history. This is also true of every human society. The forms and levels of legal plurality that we observe across different societies and over time have been extensively studied by many anthropologists and legal scholars. But, what about the intensity or degree of pluralism? Does it always stay the same or does it ever change over time? Israel is legally pluralistic today; as it was fifty-seven years ago. However, the fact that Israel has always been pluralistic does not mean that the nature, characteristics and intensity of its plurality have not changed within last six decades. Legal pluralism is the reflection of complex human interactions on our normative universe. It changes as a society evolves. With these changes in its form and structure, the degree of plurality also changes. As a result, societies constantly become 'more' or 'less' pluralistic over time.

Hence, in order to answer the question of 'how much plurality', we should be able to capture spatio-temporal variations in the degree of legal pluralism. In this regard, this paper aims to introduce a simple technique of quantification which could capture variances in the degree of legal pluralism over time and across localities. In addition the paper will also offer a number of theoretical, methodological and ontological novelties to better facilitate a diachronic analysis of legal pluralism.

## A New Perspective on Legal Pluralism

There are two types of legal pluralism: weak and strong (Griffiths 1986), or, in Woodman's terminology, state law pluralism and deep pluralism (Woodman 1999). Weak pluralism exists when the sovereign commands different bodies of law for different groups in the population by incorporating their normative orderings into the central administration of law and courts. This type of pluralism can be seen as a 'technique of governance' or a mere arrangement within state law, as the normative existence of non-state norms depends upon their recognition by the central administration (Griffiths 1986). Strong pluralism, on the other hand, resembles an inexorable state of affairs in which all normative orderings regardless of their origin and mutual recognition by one another co-exist side by side within a normative universe (Cover 1995). From this point of view, state law is just one among many other normative orderings in society. In fact, Griffiths argues that only legal pluralism in the latter form can serve as a basis for analytic and descriptive framework, as weak or state law pluralism is no more than a statement of legal doctrine, and hence irrelevant to sociological investigation. This view has been widely shared, albeit with serious reservations, among scholars (F. von Benda-Beckmann 1997; K. von Benda-Beckmann 2001; Tamanaha 1993).

Griffiths argues that the central objective of a descriptive conception of legal pluralism should be the destruction of the ideological backbone of legal centralism which is that law is a single, unified, and exclusive hierarchical normative ordering stemming from the power of the state (1986: 4-5). Such conceptualizations of legal pluralism scholarship as an intellectual crusade have led to the banishment of state law pluralism in academic circles because of their strong emphasis on anti-étatism. In fact, theories of legal pluralism with lenses focused on society have become quite fashionable among the scholars who have pioneered this field of study (Merry 1988; Snyder 1981).

The project of legal pluralism cannot be confined only to the investigation of social fields which are not penetrated by the state law. Today, in the reign of the absolute nation-state, almost no source of law, either customary or religious, can manage to stay intact (Unger 1976: 66-86). "In a legal field, there is neither absolute isolation nor absolute autonomy" (Yilmaz 1999: 73). In other words, state laws and non-state normative orderings are not two different and completely separate entities. They rather coexist in the same normative universe and dynamically interact with one another in a number of ways. From a relational perspective (Hunt 1993), state law and non-state laws are mutually constitutive (Fitzpatrick 1983, 1984; Silbey 1992). In short, as opposed to Griffiths, the instances of non-state normative orderings, incorporated within a so-called 'unified' central administration under the auspices of the state should well be construed as a remarkable instance of legal pluralism, and as a relevant sociological fact worthy of further examination.

The state-society dichotomy in the study of legal pluralism should not be exaggerated. After all, the state is a social construction. It does not exist outside of social reality; but it is part of it. The boundaries between state and society are blurred. It is almost impossible to tell where the boundaries of state end and those of society start. The distinction should be taken not as a simple border between two free-standing domains but "as a line drawn internally within the networks of institutional mechanisms through which a social and political order is maintained" (Mitchell 1991: 78). Moreover, the state is not the omnipresent, omnipotent organization that we all think; it is rather a contradictory entity that acts against itself. Understanding this paradoxical character of the state requires a dualistic approach, "one that recognizes the corporate, unified dimension of the state in its image, and one that dismantles this wholeness by means of examining its contradictory practices and alliances of its disparate parts" (Migdal 2001: 22). This is a "limited state" with a certain degree of autonomy embedded (Evans 1995: 59) in a concrete set of ties that bind the state and society together, and provide institutionalized channels for continual negotiation of the rules of the game. This constant renegotiation of the normative universe between the state and society leads to an accommodation which often takes the form of state law pluralism (Scharf and Nina 2001; Wilson 2001).

However, the phenomenon of state law pluralism has often been treated as an anachronistic legacy of colonialism (Benton 2002; Darian-Smith and Fitzpatrick 1999; Galanter and Dhavan 1989; Griffiths 1986; Hooker 1975; Larson 2001; Thompson 2000; Young 1994). According to these accounts, postcolonial states have simply continued down the same path as their colonial predecessors, and conserved the plural systems of law in their territories. Furthermore, such explanations not only consider the existence of state law pluralism as an anachronistic phenomenon, but also systematically treat the postcolonial states as disempowered and incapacitated entities which have not been able to overcome the resistance of social groups, and have weakly recognized the jurisdiction of non-state rule-making and -implementing communities (Vanderlinden 1989).

The path dependency (Mahoney and Rueschemeyer 2003; Pierson 2000, 2004; Thelen 1999) or colonial legacy approaches to the study of state law pluralism also offers a homeostatic vision of pluralism. This is mostly caused by a wholesale subscription to the Griffiths' project of anti-étatism. From this perspective, 'normative vitality' is exclusively attributed to the 'living law' which could only survive in the domain of deep legal pluralism while state law pluralism is seen as a homeostatic domain which has already lost its 'normative vitality' as a result of incorporation by the state. In addition, this strong anti-étatism has also reduced the role of the state to a mere passive and disempowered object in the creation of polycentric legal systems, as ethnographic and micro-sociological investigations have often adopted society or social formations as their unit of analysis (Snyder 1981).

This article aims to present an alternative view of legal pluralism from the state's perspective at a higher level of abstraction (Sartori 1984) through macro-sociological and comparative analysis. However, this new approach will necessitate the introduction of a new concept: *formal plurality*. It is well established that even when it is domesticated or incorporated by the state in the form of 'weak' or 'state law' pluralism, a polycentric normative universe will still continue reproducing its stronger versions under the 'implicit' recognition or purview of the state (Woodman 1999: 19). Hence, the concept of 'formal plurality' refers to the façade of state law pluralism, whereas 'informal plurality' indicates the stronger versions of state law pluralism which can be found in grey areas of the normative universe where the jurisdiction of non-state norms and institutions are subsequently acquiesced in by the state without a formal acknowledgement such as recognition or incorporation. In short, formal and informal plurality can be respectively seen as 'weak' and 'strong' versions of state law pluralism[1].

---

[1] For example, despite the fact that the Islamic law has been recognized and incorporated into the unified body of Indian family laws since the colonial times, an alternative network of Islamic Shari'a courts (*Dar-ul Qaza*) has recently emerged in some parts of the country. These courts are run by the Indian Muslims themselves, independent of government bodies. Although these courts have no official status, their existence is somewhat tolerated as alternative dispute mechanisms by the Indian state, while some of their decisions are also officially recognized as arbitration rulings by the national courts (S.T. Mahmood 2001; T. Mahmood 2002). In brief, these courts were founded as a response to popular discontent over the application of Islamic law and principles in the secular courts

Formal plurality indicates the extent to which the reality of living plurality is reflected in modern nation-states' legal systems. It is the embodiment of the state's formal response to the existing multiple normative orderings which claim to regulate the same socio-legal space simultaneously with state law. Since formal plurality is just a reverberation of living plurality in the book of the state, it should always look tidier, more organized and centralized than informal plurality, as it will also show signs of a weaker or lighter version of living plurality in degree and magnitude.

The recruitment of the concept of formal plurality helps us understand better the choices of states and answer such thorny questions as: Do states always act out of weakness and passively accept whatever form of plurality is imposed upon them by the social forces? Can modern nation-states prefer legal pluralism? Can they intentionally 'regulate' or 're-design' existing multiple jurisdictions in accordance with their ideological preferences? If they can do so, then, how can they do it? Which communal jurisdictions and policy areas do they choose to reform? What factors influence their choices of reform?

Understanding the state's role in creating or designing its version of pluralism in the form of 'formal plurality' requires a new set of tools with some theoretical, methodological and epistemological innovations. Legal pluralism (formal or informal) is an ever-changing, dynamic, living structure (Yilmaz 2005). It is not frozen in time. Neither is it a monolithic, uniform phenomenon. Hence, an innovative approach should be able to diagnose legal pluralism without neglecting the spatio-temporal differences in its structure, degree and forms (for example, between colonial and post-colonial forms of pluralism) (Sezgin 2004).

The approach that I suggest will look at the dynamic mélange of state-society relations not from a synchronic but rather from a diachronic, process-oriented perspective to understand the spatio-temporal variations in the degree, level and form of legal pluralism. Broadly speaking, it will attempt to explain variations across countries (ruled by the same colonial power), and across different groups within the same country; and variations across different policy areas and over time, in a somewhat consistent and generalizable structure. Only then could we,

---

of the Indian state. Hence, Indian formal plurality has reproduced its stronger versions in the form of informal plurality.

for example, qualitatively and quantitatively account for the changes in the structure and degrees of legal pluralisms found in colonial and postcolonial India. Or it will explain to us why we do not observe the same type, level and degree of legal pluralism across countries which share the same history (e.g. Pakistan and India). Moreover, such a theory will also explicate the differences in the degrees of legal pluralisms found across various subgroups within the same society (e.g. Hindus and Muslims in India).

However attempts at a macro-sociological theory built on a somewhat nomothetic base should not come at the expense of an acknowledgement of the intricate idiosyncrasies of a society we study. Rather we should innovate with methodological and epistemological novelties that will allow us to examine the variants and the differing degrees of legal plurality as we maintain a centered focus on the state and keep a second eye on societal structures. The "New Institutionalist theory" (Hall and Taylor 1996; North 1990, 1991) and the "state-in-society" approach (Migdal 2001) will simultaneously equip us with 'macro' and 'micro' tools that will help us find this very delicate balance, as providing a more explicit political analysis of legal pluralism by focusing both on strategic interactions between state leadership and social actors and on the broader political context in which the formation of formal plurality takes place.

## Is Quantification Possible?

A diachronic or process-oriented theory will urge us to 'quantify' and 'qualify' the phenomenon of legal pluralism so as to be able to see the changes in its structure and degree both over time and across different localities. And the problem is then how we can tackle the question of quantification. In this paper, I attempt to introduce a rather simplistic and parsimonious method to distinguish among the varying degrees of plurality.

At the outset, it must be noted that any methodology which assigns numeric values to represent non-empirical data makes a number of normative judgments. This is unavoidable and permeates much of the analysis which follows. However, once the investigator, who is in the position of making such normative judgments, has a clear understanding of the methodology employed, and knows what is measured and for what purposes, then the benefits of quantification can well outweigh its potential cost.

With this in mind, we shall use the technique of quantification to gauge the extent
to which a non-state normative ordering is incorporated within a unified legal
system. In other words, the score of pluralization that we aim to compute can be
also read as a ratio of unification, integration, or fragmentation within the context
of formal plurality. For experimental purposes, we carry out the task of
quantification on a model of personal status regime[2] as it exemplifies a strong
instance of formal plurality. We would assume that each non-state normative order
within a personal status regime is simply composed of three major elements: code
(or substantive norms), judge and court. These three elements are translated into
two distinct component variables in this study: *Code* stands on its own, while the
other two components are put into a single combined variable of *Judge/Court*, as
they are intimately interrelated. These variables are also operationalized to
facilitate valid and reliable measurement. Hence, to measure or quantify the
plurality of a particular legal system, we specifically need to decide by looking at
every single communal jurisdiction in the country, which is officially recognized
and incorporated: first whether the court system of this jurisdiction is absorbed
into a unified hierarchy of national courts; *second*, whether the legal code of this
jurisdiction applied by the courts is codified (that is, written) and territorially
unified; and lastly, whether the judges who sit on the bench are trained, salaried,
and appointed by the central government and will rule on a case regardless of the
identity of a particular litigant.

Table 1 operationalizes each variable by situating it on a continuum of
unification/fragmentation. A score of 0 for a variable on the table will attest to a
fully unified territorial administration of law and courts, whereas a score of 100

---

[2] By 'personal status regime' I refer to a single polity with several bodies of law in
which every individual will be subject to her faith's communal jurisdiction in
regard to matters of personal status such as marriage, divorce, maintenance and
inheritance. The existing family law regime of Israel, where fourteen different
ethno-religious communities' jurisdiction over their members' matters of personal
status are recognized by the government, is a great example of such regimes. The
structure and characteristics of personal law systems also vary from place to place.
In some countries, non-state normative orderings will be fully recognized and
incorporated including their norms and court-like structures (institutional
recognition), whereas in some countries the recognition will just be confined to
normative recognition, as only religious and customary norms of communities will
be codified and integrated into a national system.

Table 1: Operationalization Table

| CODE: | % |
|---|---|
| Subject to unified, codified law (same uniform territorial state law for every group; fully codified norms) | 0 |
| Subject to unified, partially codified law (same uniform territorial state law for every group; norms partially codified, some unwritten, customary norms recognised | 12.5 |
| Subject to unified, un-codified law (same uniform territorial state law for every group; uncodified norms) | 25.0 |
| Subject to partially-unified, codified law (law unified for some groups and regions; fully codified norms) | 37.5 |
| Subject to partially-unified, partially-codified law (law unified for some groups and regions; norms partially codified, some unwritten, customary norms recognised) | 50.0 |
| Subject to partially-unified, un-codified state law (law unified for some groups and regions; uncodified norms) | 62.5 |
| Subject to non-unified, codified law (Communal law – every group has its own particular set of norms; norms fully codified) | 75.0 |
| Subject to non-unified, partially-codified law (Communal law – every group has its own particular set of norms; norms partially codified, some unwritten, customary norms recognised) | 87.5 |
| Subject to non-unified, uncodified law (Communal law – every group has its own particular set of norms; uncodified norms) | 100.0 |
| | |
| JUDGES/COURTS: | % |
| Fully centralized state court (with state-trained/appointed/salaried judges for everyone) | 0 |
| State court with different state-trained/appointed/salaried judges for litigants from different groups | 12.5 |
| State court with communal divisions (structural divisions such as circuits) | 25.0 |
| State court that recruits communal experts | 37.5 |
| State court that requires endorsement from communal authorities for further legal impact within communal hierarchy | 50.0 |
| Communal courts with state representatives | 62.5 |
| Communal courts whose rulings require state endorsement | 75.0 |
| Communal courts administered by the government (with communal judges appointed/salaried by the state | 87.5 |
| Fully autonomous communal courts (with communal judges appointed/salaried by the community | 100.0 |

will manifest the total disunification or fragmentation of the court structure and law administration in the country. Between the extreme situations with scores of 0 and 100 there exist seven other possible forms that non-state law and institutions could take in their every-day interactions with the state law.

Let us explain how this whole process of computation works through an example. Let us imagine a country, X, with formal plurality. In other words, suppose that country X has recognized and incorporated the jurisdiction of two distinct ethno-religious communities (A, B) in matters of family law or personal status (which is confined to areas of Marriage and Divorce, Inheritance, and Maintenance for purposes of this study). To calculate the degree of formal plurality for the entire country in the field of personal status law, we need to look for a description that will best approximate features of each policy area (of Marriage and Divorce, Inheritance, Maintenance) in terms of its component variables (Law; Judge/Courts) on Table 1. Then we fill in each Policy Area/Component grid on Table 2, by copying its corresponding numerical value ranging from 0 to 100 from Table 1.

Thus, if Community A's communal law in regard to matters of marriage and divorce is recognized and incorporated into country X's national legal system, the communal law is 'non-unified' in the sense that there is no uniform law territorially applicable in regard to matters of marriage and divorce. Rather, every ethno-religious community has its own particularistic norms which are recognized by the central administration. As we see in its real world applications, whenever such ethno-religious systems are recognized, this recognition is often extended to include not only the codified parts of the communal law but also some of its oral and customary practices. This non-unified, partially-codified communal law is applied in the national courts by judges who are trained, appointed and salaried by the government. Let us further assume that the rulings of these courts require endorsement by the communal institutions to produce enforceable legal results within the community (e.g. approval of divorce decrees, issued by civil courts, by ecclesiastical authorities may be required if the parties involved wish to re-marry in church). Similarly, in regard to matters of maintenance, the non-unified, partially codified communal law is also applied by the government-trained-and-salaried judges at the fully centralized national courts; but in this case their rulings do not require the approval of the communal institutions. The same national judges and courts also apply the inheritance laws of different communities which are partially unified and partially codified. In other words, unlike marriage and divorce laws, inheritance laws are somewhat unified across different communities or regions. Having carefully scrutinized each variable and found a corresponding value for its descriptive features on Table 1, we should now proceed to assign the values 87.5, 50, and 87.5 to the Marriage and Divorce/Code; Inheritance/Code and Maintenance/Code cells respectively. By the same token, for the Marriage and Divorce/Judge-Court, Inheritance/Judge-Court and Maintenance/ Judge-Court cells we should fill in 50, 0, and 0 respectively.

Table 2: Country X, Component Scores

|  | Marriage/Divorce | Inheritance | Maintenance |  |
|---|---|---|---|---|
| Community A | 87.5 | 50 | 87.5 | Code |
|  | 50 | 0 | 0 | Judge/Court |
|  |  |  |  |  |
| Community B | 87.5 | 50 | 87.5 | Code |
|  | 0 | 0 | 0 | Judge/Court |

As the next step, we should take the total of individual component scores across policy areas. For example, for the Code variable, the total will be 87.5 + 50 + 87.5 = 225; the Judge/Court variable will add up to 50 (i.e., 50 + 0 + 0). Each of these totals should also be divided by three in order to calculate their average or arithmetic mean. The arithmetic means of individual component variables will give us the *Componentwise Degree of Pluralism* (CDP) scores. CDP scores can equally be equally seen as a score of decentralization or fragmentation for each component. In our example for Community A, these scores will be

$$\text{Code} = \frac{87.5 + 50 + 87.5}{3} = 75\%; \text{ and Judge/Court} = \frac{50 + 0 + 0}{3} = 17\%$$

These scores mean that country X's court structure in the field of personal laws is relatively unified across different ethno-religious groups (with a score of 17%) while the laws applied by these courts are highly decentralized or pluralized (75%).

Moreover, the arithmetic mean of these two scores will give us another very important ratio, the *Degree of Communal Autonomy* (DCA) in matters of personal status. This score - ranging between 0 and 100% - will indicate the extent to which a particular community's personal laws are integrated into or independent from the unified national family law system. For Community A, the DCA score will be:

$$DCA = \frac{75+17}{2} = 44\%$$

In order to calculate our overall *Degree of Formal Pluralism* (DFP) score for Country X, we first need to calculate the same DCA score for Community B also:

$$Code = \frac{87.5+50+87.5}{3} = \textbf{75\%}; \; Judge/Court = \frac{0+0+0}{3} = 0\%$$

$$\text{Therefore DCA for Community B} = \frac{75+0}{2} = 38\%.$$

**The DFP** score will indicate the overall degree of centralization, unification or pluralization of a particular legal system. For example, for country X, the DFP score can be worked out by taking the arithmetic mean of DCA scores for Communities A and B. Therefore,

$$DFP = \frac{44+38}{2} = 41\%$$

By comparing DFP scores across two different points in time we can determine whether a normative universe has become more fragmented or more unified over time. For example, in order to answer the question that we posed at the beginning of this paper, whether Israel was more pluralistic in 2005 than in 1948, it is necessary to find Israel's DFP scores from those two years. DFP scores could also help those students of legal pluralism who wish to undertake more macro-sociological and cross-national analyses to reach some theoretical generalizations and compare different legal systems at a higher level of abstraction. For example, we could calculate the DFP scores for both Pakistan and India in order to compare the changes in their individual scores from 1947 to 2005. Since they started from the same point we should be able, current DFP scores in hand, to tell how each country has performed. If we find that one country has lagged behind the other in terms of either its fragmentation or its centralization scores, this would surely pose a very interesting puzzle for any investigator with a serious interest in the study of legal pluralism.

Lastly, another very useful score - the *Policywise Degree of Plurality* (PDP), could be computed by taking the arithmetic mean of individual component scores within each policy area. For example, for the field of marriage and divorce in Community A:

$$PDP = \frac{87.5 + 50}{2} = 68.75\% \text{ for Community A (Marriage and Divorce)}^3$$

To calculate the overall DFP score for the entire country, we also need to calculate the same score for community B. Thereafter, we again take the arithmetic mean of community A's and community B's PDP scores to produce the nationwide PDP score:

$$PDP = \frac{87.5 + 0}{2} = 43.75\% \text{ for Community B (Marriage and Divorce),}^4 \text{ and}$$

$$PDP = \frac{68.75 + 43.75}{2} = 56.25\% \text{ for Country X (Marriage/Divorce)}$$

The PDP will tell us to what extent a particular policy area is centralized or fragmented across the different legal communities within the same country. By the

---

[3] In the same way, Community A's PDP scores for the maintenance and inheritance fields could be calculated as:

PDP (Maintenance) = (87.5 + 0) ÷ 2 = 43.75%;
PDP (Inheritance) = (50 + 0) ÷ 2 = 25%.

[4] Similarly, Community B's PDP scores for maintenance and inheritance fields will be:

PDP (Maintenance) = (87.5 + 0) ÷ 2 = 43.75%
PDP (Inheritance) = (50 + 0) ÷ 2 = 25 %

same token, we could also determine which policy area, in which community, is more centralized or fragmented. For example, in both communities A and B above, we see that inheritance laws are much more unified and centralized than both the marriage and divorce and the maintenance laws. These findings will automatically lead to such questions as: Why are the inheritance laws more centralized than the laws of marriage and divorce? Does it mean that the field of inheritance is more heavily regulated by the central administration and that the central administration has a particular interest in this policy area? What are dynamics of state-society relations in regard to rules of inheritance? What about comparing PDP scores across different communities? What if we find that marriage and divorce rules are more centralized in community B than A (meaning that B will have a lower PDP score in the field of marriage and divorce, as in our example)? Further, after a combined reading of these PDP scores with each community's DCA scores, what might be said about the relative balance of power between the different communities and the central state administration? If we find that community A also enjoys a higher ratio of DCA, could we say that community A has more autonomy in this field because it commanded a better bargaining position vis-à-vis the state at the time of incorporation?

## Benefits of Quantification

The degree of formal plurality will range from 0% to 100%, both of which resemble ideal types. A DFP score of 100 % will exemplify an extreme version of formal plurality, as a score of 0% will point to the existence of extremely powerful centralist and monistic institutions and practices put in place by the state.

In the existing literature, state law pluralism and its variants, mostly in the form of personal status regimes, have often been portrayed as a timeless and static phenomenon. This has rendered the comparative analysis of such normative systems across localities, communities, policy areas and time impossible. However, the theoretical approach and the method of quantification that I have proposed here should make the cross spatio-temporal analysis of legal pluralism a possibility. For example, Country X's degree of plurality in the field of family law is 41%. In addition, we could calculate the degree of plurality at some other point in time and compare it with the current score of 41%. Hence, the comparison of two ratios measured at two different points in time will help us discover the temporal changes in the structure and form of pluralism within the same country. Or the comparison of degrees of plurality measured in different countries can help us explain cross-national variations. Moreover, we could also categorize countries based on their DFP scores such as countries with high degree (67-100%), medium degree (34-66%) and low degree (0-33%) pluralism. We could then try to correlate these scores with some common characteristics widely shared across countries within the same category. For example, if we study personal status regimes in a cross-national sample and find that countries with high DFP scores also exhibit strong theocratic tendencies, then we could perhaps nomothetically infer that all theocratic regimes will denote high degrees of formal plurality.

Cross national and temporal analyses will also aid us to closely study the performances of various governments in reforming their legal systems. First, by looking at their componentwise plurality scores over time, we could analyze how national governments regulated their formal plurality: whether they attempted to unify the codes of various communities or centralize the national court structures, as in the case of Egypt which absorbed the religious courts of various communities into the national court system while leaving these communities' laws non-unified under a central administration (Law No: 462 of 1955). Likewise, the comparison of degrees of autonomy across sub-national communities should also tell us a great deal about the relationship of states with various ethno-religious groups under their rule. The example of Country X above starkly exposes these differences across various communities within the same polity, leading to the question, why is there such a difference between the two communities' autonomy scores? The reading of communal autonomy scores along with such scores as policywise plurality and componentwise plurality scores, we could better elaborate on communal differences. For instance, we may see that central governments are more active in undertaking procedural reforms than more substantive reforms, since they can with relative ease alter the court structures but not the norms of certain communities for pragmatic reasons. Or, as was the case in Israel, governments may prefer stricter regulation of some policy areas directly related to the exchange of land and capital, such as inheritance and maintenance, over such sensitive issues as marriage and divorce. Eventually, spatio-temporal analysis of formal plurality may also demonstrate whether variations in the degrees of autonomy, shown by componentwise or policywise scores across different ethno-religious groups, have become more or less visible along the lines of national majorities and minorities since independence, as is the case in India.

As a final note, an investigator should always keep it in mind that the feasibility and reliability of this technique of quantification is limited in several ways: First, like any other research project, it is limited by its database. The technique can be used as a tool of analysis only if there is hard data in the hands of the researcher. As seen, the operationalization of variables entails an extensive amount of data which can be gathered only through ethnographic research. This means that the study of legal pluralism still primarily relies upon the collection of primary and secondary data through field research. Second, this paper has offered a simplified and parsimonious vision of formal plurality. But in reality, formal plurality could also get as messy and tricky as informal plurality. We frequently find that the nature of the relationship between state law and non-state law may not be straightforward. Both state and non-state normative orderings may enjoy concurrent jurisdictions in some policy areas. For example, in Israel individuals have an option to take their maintenance or inheritance related matters to either a religious court or a civil family court. In such cases it may not always be very clear how to operationalize the variables of code or court and judge. Thus the investigator who has a good understanding of the actual legal practices in a society and is knowledgeable about the formal legal structure, should have the flexibility to modify the model to meet the practical needs of his research.

# References

BENDA-BECKMANN, Franz von
1997    'Citizens, strangers and indigenous peoples: conceptual politics and legal pluralism.' *Law & Anthropology* 9: 1-42.
BENDA-BECKMANN, Keebet von
2001    'Legal pluralism.' *Tai Culture*, 6: 18-40.
BENTON, L.
2002    *Law and Colonial Cultures. Legal Regimes in World History, 1400-1900.* New York: Cambridge University Press.
COVER, R.
1995    'Nomos and narrative.' Pp. 95-172 in M. Minow, M. Ryan and A. Sarat (eds.), *Narrative, Violence and the Law*. Ann Arbor: The University of Michigan Press.
DARIAN-SMITH, E., and P. FITZPATRICK (eds.)
1999    *Laws of the Postcolonial.* Ann Arbor: The University of Michigan Press.
EVANS, P. B.
1995    *Embedded Autonomy: States and Industrial Transformation.* Princeton, N.J.: Princeton University Press.

FITZPATRICK, Peter
1983    'Law, plurality and underdevelopment.' Pp. 159-182 in D. Sugarman (ed.), *Legality, Ideology and the State*. London: Academic Press.
1984    'Law and Societies.' *Osgoode Hall Law Journel* 22: 115-138.
GALANTER, Marc and R. DHAVAN
1989    *Law and Society in Modern India*. Delhi ; New York: Oxford University Press.
GRIFFITHS, John
1986    'What is Legal Pluralism?' *Journal of Legal Pluralism* 24: 1-55.
HALL, P.A.. and R.C.R. Taylor
1996    'Political Science and the three new institutionalisms.' *Political Studies* 44: 936-957.
HOOKER, M. B.
1975    *Legal Pluralism: An Introduction to Colonial and Neo-Colonial Laws*. Oxford: Clarendon Press.
HUNT, A.
1993    *Explorations in Law and Society: Toward A Constitutive Theory of Law*. New York: Routledge.
LARSON, G.J.
2001    *Religion and Personal Law in Secular India: A Call to Judgment*. Bloomington: Indiana University Press.
MAHMOOD, S.T.
2001    'The Shari'at courts in modern India.' Unpublished Paper.
MAHMOOD, T.
2002    *The Muslim law of India* (3rd ed.). New Delhi: LexisNexis.
MAHONEY, J. and D. RUESCHEMEYER
2003    *Comparative Historical Analysis in the Social Sciences*. Cambridge, U.K., New York: Cambridge University Press.
MERRY, S.E.
1988    'Legal Pluralism.' *Law & Society Review* 22: 869-896.
MIGDAL, J.S.
2001    *State in Society: Studying How States and Societies Transform and Constitute One Another*. New York: Cambridge University Press.
MITCHELL, T.
1991    'The limits of the state: beyond statist approaches and their critics.' *American Political Science Review* 85: 77-96.
NORTH, D.
1990    *Institutions, Institutional Change and Economic Performance*. Cambridge: Cambridge University Press.

1991      'Institutions.' *Journal of Economic Perspectives* 5: 97-112.
PIERSON, P.
2000      'Increasing returns, path dependency, and the study of politics.' *American Political Science Review* 94: 251-267.
2004      *Politics in Time: History, Institutions, and Social Analysis*. Princeton, N.J.: Princeton University Press.
SARTORI, G.
1984      'Guidelines for concept analysis.' Pp. 15-88 in G. Sartori (ed.), *Social Science Concepts: A Systematic Analysis*. Beverly Hills: Sage.
SCHARF, W., and D. NINA,
2001      *The Other Law: Non-State Ordering in South Africa*. Lansdowne: Juta.
SEZGIN, Y.
2004      'A political account for legal confrontation between state and society: the case of Israeli legal pluralism.' Pp. 199-235 in A. Sarat and P. Ewick (eds.), *Studies in Law, Politics, and Society* 32. Amsterdam: Elsevier.
SILBEY, S.S.
1992      'Making a place for cultural analyses of law.' *Law & Social Inquiry* 17: 39-48.
SNYDER, F.
1981      'Anthropology, dispute processes and law: a critical introduction.' *British Journal of Law & Society* 8: 141-180.
TAMANAHA, B.Z.
1993      'The folly of the "social scientific" concept of legal pluralism.' *Journal of Law and Society* 20: 192-217.
THELEN, K.
1999      'Historical institutionalism in comparative politics.' *Annual Review of Political Science* 2: 369-404.
THOMPSON, E.
2000      *Colonial Citizens: Republican Rights, Paternal Privilege, and Gender in French Syria and Lebanon*. New York: Columbia University Press.
UNGER, R.M.
1976      *Law in Modern Society*. New York: The Free Press.
VANDERLINDEN, J.
1989      'Return to legal pluralism: twenty years later.' *Journal of Legal Pluralism* 28: 149-157.
WILSON, R.
2001      *The Politics of Truth and Reconciliation in South Africa: Legitimizing the Post-Apartheid State*. Cambridge, New York: Cambridge University Press.

WOODMAN, G.R.
1999    'The idea of legal pluralism.' Pp. 3-19 in B. Dupret, M. Berger and L.
        al-Zwaini (eds.), *Legal Pluralism in the Arab World*. The Hague: Kluwer
        Law International.
YILMAZ, I.
1999    *Dynamic Legal Pluralism and The Reconstruction of Unofficial Muslim
        Laws in England, Turkey and Pakistan*. Unpublished PhD Dissertation,
        SOAS, University of London.
2005    *Muslim Laws, Politics and Society in Modern Nation States: Dynamic
        Legal Pluralisms in England, Turkey and Pakistan*. Aldershot: Ashgate.
YOUNG, C.
1994    *The African Colonial State in Comparative Perspective*. New Haven: Yale
        University Press.

# THE HINDU SUCCESSION ACT:
# ONE LAW, PLURAL IDENTITIES[1]

Karine Bates

## Introduction[2]

Issues of gender and legal pluralism are complex and multidimensional, and thus require varied research strategies. Recent ethnographic and comparative studies reveal the significance of property rights in shaping gender inequality. Ursula Sharma's (1980) study of two villages in Northwest India was the first to examine women's access to property in this region. However, data on gender and property

---

[1] This paper is based on my Ph.D. thesis, submitted to the Department of Anthropology, McGill University, 2005. The research on which this paper is based was funded by the *Social Sciences and Humanities Research Council of Canada*, the Alma Matter Fund of McGill University, the *Centre for Society, Technology and Development* (Department of Anthropology, McGill University) and the *McGill Centre for Research and Teaching on Women*. Another part of the funding for my research comes from the Government of India (GoI) through the India Studies Program of the *Shastri Indo-Canadian Institute* (SICI). Neither the GoI nor the SICI nor other granting agencies necessarily endorse the views expressed herein.

[2] I would like to thank my thesis supervisor Professor Donald W. Attwood for his inspiring guidance throughout my Master's and Ph.D. research. Also, I would like to thank Professor Laurel Bossen for always being there for me. Special thanks to Professor Jane Glenn of the McGill Faculty of Law for her continuous support. Finally, my thanks to Melissa Bull who helped, through her many revisions, shape my paper.

rights are scattered among studies of other topics. Significant recent exceptions include Bina Agarwal's (1994) book on women and property rights, Martha Chen's (1998 and 2000) books on widows, and recently the first intensive local case study of women and property rights conducted by Srimati Basu in New Delhi (Basu 1999). These investigations clearly demonstrate that understanding women's access and rights to land, and other forms of property, is a key element in the study of women's status. Also, these studies confirm women's marginal land and property ownership, despite legal reforms (Agarwal 1994; Chen and Drèze 1995; Chen 2000).

My research draws on data collected through intensive field research in Bheema, a village of the Pune district, in the state of Maharashtra. It is complemented by legal research on statutes, case law, and court procedures. I focus on widows in rural Maharashtra in order to analyze how legal reforms, as well as social and economic changes, influence their entitlement to property. Another objective is to provide depth and add a new dimension to multidisciplinary research in India, by focusing on property rights in Maharashtra, a region relatively neglected by social scientists and anthropologists.

Finally, this study undertakes comparative analysis of socio-economic, as well as regional variations, in the ability of a widow to claim her legal property rights and cope in other ways, thereby deepening our understanding of the interaction of legal reforms, socio-economic trends, and customary law.

## 1. Methodology: the Elaboration of a Socio-Legal Ethnography

In order to understand how Indian women interact with various perceptions of social order and modes of conflict resolution, it is important to investigate key elements of their lives such as household dynamics, kinship systems, marriage rules, economic resources, inheritance patterns, gender socialization, caste organization and concepts of rights and duties. In addition, to explain access to property rights and the legal system, it is necessary to examine how the social status and legal status of women are both changing in Maharashtra. Ethnographic accounts provide concrete examples of the way women cope with crises during particularly vulnerable phases of the life-cycle, such as widowhood.

My fourteen months of fieldwork in India was composed of two interrelated phases. The first, starting in March 2001, consisted of intensive ethnographic research, while during the second, from September 2001 until May 2002, I undertook legal analysis in addition to ethnographic research. During each phase, I combined ethnographic research techniques with methods generally used by legal anthropologists. Various forms of data collection were adapted and re-shaped according to the requirements of both the research objectives and the research participants.[3]

I stayed in the village of Bheema[4] for four months (March to July 2001), during which I conducted interviews with thirty-five women and their families, fourteen of the women being widows. Men also participated in my study, which enabled me to explore further nuances of gender issues, married life, and inheritance practices. Accompanied by a research assistant, I visited these people regularly during my four months in Bheema, and also in the following nine months when I was based in Pune for the second phase of my research. As well as conducting interviews, I collected through informal discussions individual life stories, family histories, and some marriage and inheritance genealogies. This data is of the type on which the narratives presented by Anne Griffiths through life histories were based. As she writes, these narratives

> ... portray village people's perceptions of law, the circumstances under which they do or do not have access to formal legal forums, and, in particular, the conditions under which individuals find themselves silenced or unable to negotiate with others in terms of day-to-day life. (Griffiths 2002: 161)

Participant observation provided a way to contextualize the information obtained

---

[3] My sincere thanks to the Apte family who made me feel at home in Pune and who were so generous helping me with my research. I would like to thank the people of the village of Bheema who, with great generosity, welcomed me into their community during my fieldwork in India. Similarly, I am indebted to all the people in Pune who invited me into their homes, thereby allowing me to witness most aspects of Maharashtrian society. I would also like to thank my Research Assistant, Mira, for her generous collaboration on my fieldwork project.

[4] I have given the village the fictitious name of Bheema in order to preserve the anonymity of the people who were generous enough to share their knowledge and life experiences with me.

through talking with respondents. The participants in the study belonged to different castes, classes and age groups and had different levels of education. The widows had lost their husbands to various causes, such as accidents, old age and disease. To facilitate comparison of the data collected through fieldwork in Bheema, I conducted additional interviews with 30 women (including 12 widows) from several other villages in Pune district.

The data collected through fieldwork was complemented by legal research, specifically the analysis of statutes, jurisprudence, legislative records, court procedures and cases. Because so few widows go to court to claim their inheritance rights and the *Hindu Succession Act* (hereafter HSA) is seldom used, I found it useful to observe non-widowed women and men in Pune's District and Family Courts. The court disputes observed were directly related to property issues in cases of alimony, land partition, pension claims and marriage registration certificates, and indirectly related in cases of separation and divorce.

Furthermore, since access to justice is highly procedural, it was instructive to investigate case preparation between lawyers and clients. One lawyer opened her office to me and allowed me to observe her interactions with clients. There I was able to explore widows', non-widows', and men's interpretations and understandings of the law, their opinions on whether widows should claim their property rights, and their general views on the condition of widows. It was useful to meet with those persons to obtain further information concerning their relationship with the legal system because only one of the widows interviewed in the village had actually gone to court to claim her inheritance rights. Alternative mechanisms of conflict resolution were studied through the follow up of various cases heard by the social workers and women's rights organization.

Overall, this methodology allowed me to explore the broader social context of widowhood, the reasons why widows do not claim their inheritance rights under the *Hindu Succession Act* and the elements that make up access to justice.

## 2. The Hindu Succession Act of 1956: Modifying Social Roles and Reorganizing Kinship

The study of women's property rights in India is particularly pertinent when we consider how many of the post-independence legal reforms are the results of the cohabitation of various legal traditions. Like other national laws concerning the personal rights of the Hindu population, the HSA is the result of a compromise between different legal traditions, such as various Hindu schools of law, Hindu legal patterns, British common law and the Western philosophy underlying the concept of equality. The long debate over personal laws that took place in the 1950s led Indian legislators to envisage a new 'social order' in their laws, which consequently became potential agents for social change. But such legislative initiatives are not sufficient because their success depends on the reactions of tribunals along with their capacity and/or desire to elaborate a new jurisprudence. In addition, innovative legal cases depend on people's knowledge of the law and their desire to use it instead of other forms of conflict resolution.

One of the most important ideologies of the Western philosophy of law is its particular conception of equality, a concept that has been implemented in different ways by the diverse national legal systems in the West. In India, this ideology was introduced and then transformed, in the philosophies of certain charismatic political leaders prior to the country's independence, namely Gandhi, Tagore and to some extent Nehru, who all promoted the ideal of increased equality among the castes (Dandekar 1986: 23).

After Independence, rights to equality became an integral part of the fundamental rights of the Indian Constitution. Three articles in the Constitution specify the scope of the fundamental right to equality: Article 14 is concerned with equality before the law, Article 15 expresses the prohibition of discrimination based on religion, race, caste, birthplace and sex, and Article 16 outlines equality of opportunity in public employment (Béteille 1986: 123).

Although the principle of individual rights entrenched in the Constitution may be inspired by a Western legal tradition that associates equality with individualism, the concept of equality in India may be different. For example, the man who led the framing of the Constitution, Ambedkar, spoke strongly in support of the individual, but he also pleaded for and obtained the recognition of special rights to specific groups, such as the Scheduled tribes and castes. According to Ambedkar, "[w]hat was at issue was not simply equality as a right available to all individuals but also equality as a policy aimed at bringing about certain changes in the structure of society." (Béteille 1986: 126) According to Béteille the Indian perspective differs from the more individualistic view of the Western concept of equality.

The same makers of the Constitution refused to have one uniform civil code by which women could enjoy equal rights within the family, because the code might then interfere with the religious rights of various communities. In this they echoed what the British rulers had said when they refused to have one civil code for India. Nowadays, in the absence of a uniform civil code, women and men are governed by different legislation depending on their religion.[5]

Even though the Indian Government has expressed interest in the idea of women becoming equal to men, very few legislative initiatives have been taken regarding the property rights of Hindu women. The major exception to this is the HSA, enacted in 1956, which legislates for Hindus in cases of intestate succession.[6] Since one of its goals was to stop gender-based discrimination, women received some access to the property of their deceased fathers or husbands.

However, this legislation only provides for a limited equality of succession rights for Hindu women (Agarwal 1994: 211-212; Agnes 1999: 82).[7] The following case illustrates its possible applications. Take a Hindu family composed of a husband, his wife and three children (two sons and one daughter). If the husband dies before the other family members, then his acquired or self-accumulated property will be divided into four equal parts: one for the widow and one for each child, both male and female.[8] But the ancestral property will not be divided equally among the female and male members of the family. A detailed review of the Act is beyond the scope of this paper. What is important to acknowledge is that the national law had maintained the longstanding division between ancestral and acquired property prevailing in many Hindu communities.

---

[5] The HSA applies to all Hindus, Buddhists, Sikhs and Jains (but not to Scheduled Tribes - unless otherwise indicated by the Central Government).

[6] Section 3(g) of the *HSA*: "intestate" – a person is deemed to die intestate in respect of property of which he or she has not made a testamentary disposition capable of taking effect. It is important to note that testamentary disposition are seldom in a village like Bheema, even in materially affluent families.

[7] According to the *HSA*, the preferential heirs of a Hindu male is his children (daughters and sons), his widow and his mother. They are part of what the Act refer to as Class 1 heirs. The father of an Hindu male is not a "preferential heir."

[8] Ancestral property cannot be willed away by the father.

Ancestral property is formed in the following way. In Maharashtra, prior to Independence and the HSA, the inheritance pattern was patrilineal and the Mitakshara was the predominant school of law. Under Mitakshara, the property was divided among male heirs *per stirpes* (between branches) and not *per capita* (Attwood 1995). This *per stirpes* division led to the creation of a coparcenary.

> Under the Mitakshara law, the property of a Hindu male devolved through survivorship jointly upon four generations of male heirs. The ownership was by birth and not by succession. Upon his birth, the male member acquired the right to property (Agnes 1999: 14).

Under this coparcenary system, the widow could only take a limited interest, called the widow's estate, which meant that she had no power to dispose of the *corpus* of the property (except in certain cases). In practice, the widow really depended upon her sons to take care of her and ethnographies report numerous cases of abandoned widows. Post-Independence legislation tried to put an end to this; however, the HSA does not grant daughters and widows full property rights in a coparcenary because they are not considered to be part of the coparcenary as men are by birth.

The Indian Constitution allows each state to modify personal laws. In 1994, the Government of Maharashtra took further steps to enhance women's access to property. Following reports from the National Commission for Women, the Government of Maharashtra elaborated its 'Policy for Women', whose explicit goal:

> ... is to ensure an improvement in the physical, mental and emotional quality of life of the women of the State. This goal will be attained through ensuring equality for women in every sphere of life, but specially in political, economical, social, emotional and cultural areas.... In order to achieve these goals, the Government recognizes the need to evaluate existing traditions and ideas on societal roles and relationships existing between men and women, and accepts the responsibility to assist organizations and individuals to alter them in keeping with the needs and realities of today's society (GoM 1994: 5).

In section 8 on *Women and Law* of this policy, the Maharashtra State Government recognizes that: "The opportunity to obtain redressal of grievance through recourse to the law is the fundamental right of every citizen. For most women, however, this opportunity has remained largely on paper." In line with the policy, the HSA was amended to give women access to coparcenary rights. Thus Maharashtra, like Karnataka, Andhra Pradesh, and Tamil Nadu, has adopted more progressive laws that allow women to obtain a share in both the acquired and the ancestral property of the father or husband.[9]

The HSA Amendment of September 2005 has entrenched the progressive trends found in the southern states into the national law. The effects of this law providing women coparcenary rights have yet to be seen. What we learn through ethnographic research is that, in n practice, despite progressive initiatives by the State of Maharashtra, the HSA is not used by the people, female or male. The limited success of the HSA can be explained by a complex interplay of factors. Inspired by the ideology of 'equality' as framed in Western philosophy, and by a desire to respect some Hindu legal schools (mainly the Mitakshara), the HSA was the result of combining two legal systems that are partially at odds with one another. Furthermore, this Act was a legislative initiative that had to be implemented in a rapidly changing young nation whose centuries-old history had been characterized by various phases of cultural and religious invasions and colonization. In addition, local and regional practices have often modified the impact written laws have had on different Hindu legal schools of thought. It is in this context of legal pluralism that the policy-makers of independent India elaborated laws for the new state, hence establishing a new social order concerning access to property.

Property rights are so crucial to one's place in society that the HSA has the potential to modify many aspects of a woman's life. By giving inheritance rights to daughters and widows this act proposes a radically different organization of the ideal household, which is commonly referred to as 'the Indian joint family'. This joint family, that is both patrilineal and virilocal, consists in two or more married couples, which means that senior parents live with their sons as well as the wives and children of their sons. The traditional ideal to which every Hindu and his wife aspire is to have a household composed of themselves, several sons, and their wives and children (Shah 1988: 35). The daughter stays with the household until

---

[9] In Kerala, it is the legal concept of joint family that has been abolished, rendering the issue of coparcenary rights by birth irrelevant.

she is married and afterwards her periodic visits to the natal household are also part of this ideal (Shah 1988: 35). After marriage, she belongs to her in-laws' family and, as we will see, the daughters do not want to cause problems to her parents and brothers even after her patrilocal move.

However, very few households achieve this goal for various reasons (Shah 1988: 36). The deviations from the norm are often caused by demographic accident and lack of opportunity (Attwood 1995: 4). First, the couple may be childless. Secondly, the couple may only have daughters. Thirdly, they may only have one son. Finally, even if the couple has many sons, they may separate. Indeed, the establishment of separate households by the sons is one of the major phases of dispersal of the Indian family (Shah 1988), although it does not always mean that they have given up joint control of family property (Shah 1974: 30). Even if there are separate households during the parents' lifetime, the sons and parents still constitute a single 'family'. Competition and inequality among brothers may provoke partition (Attwood 1995). "Members of a lineage are supposed to be equal, but villagers are acutely aware that the relationship is fraught with competition and potential hostility" (Carter 1974: 91-92). On the other hand, fraternal co-operation may also lead to greater efficiency, leading to the expansion of assets (Attwood 1995: 12).

In her study of women's difficulties in using the legal system in Botswana, Anne Griffiths relates that various forms of power "differ on the basis of gender, but also vary between members of the same sex and across generations" (Griffiths 2002: 175). In addition, like property rights and legal interpretations of succession rights, the joint family has always been subject to regional variations.

## 3. The Study of Property Rights and Widowhood in a Context of Regional Variations

Barbara Miller (1981) initiated the comparative study of female experience in rural India. She found that women tend to be vulnerable in certain phases of their life cycle, specifically in early childhood, the early stages of marriage and widowhood. This finding is supported by Bina Agarwal's (1994) comparative analysis of women and property rights in South Asia. Martha Chen's (2000) research shows that widows are placed in an even more precarious situation if they cannot claim property devolved from parents or ex-husbands. Scattered data confirm that, in rural Maharashtra, widows sometimes face problems in claiming rights to their deceased husbands' property (Dandekar 1986; Attwood 1995, n.d.).

Agarwal has noted the difficulty in constructing a comparative regional analysis of women and property rights, given the general lack of ethnographic data on this topic (1994: 4647). There is significant variation between regions, like the contrasts between North and South India that have been extensively discussed (e.g. Caldwell et al. 1988; Drèze and Sen 1997; Dyson and Moore 1983; Jeffery et al. 1989, 1996, 1997; Maclachlan 1993; Miller 1981; Minturn 1993; Wadley 1994). Yet gender inequality in Western India has largely not been explored by most social scientists.

Legal reforms related to property rights in Maharashtra tend to follow a southern pattern[10] of progressive legal and social movements. Yet, with northern patterns of patrilineal inheritance, patrilocal residence, and increasing dowry practices,[11] how are these progressive laws perceived and understood by its population?

Maharashtra is a compelling location to study for its regional variations because, on the one hand, Maharashtra has a leading position within the Indian context in terms of economic development, urbanization, and social reforms. On the other

---

[10] I refer to Sen to define the northern patterns as including the states of Harayana, Himachal Pradesh, Punjab, Rajasthan, Uttar Pradesh (Sen et al 1997). Agarwal designates these states as being part of the North-West pattern and includes Jammu and Kashmir (Agarwal 1994). Both Sen and Agarwal consider Andhra Pradesh, Karnataka, Kerala, Tamil Nadu as the states forming the southern model. In addition, according to Agarwal, the following states of Norh-East India follow, such as in the South of India, socio-economic patterns that gives women better access to property: Arunachal Pradesh, Assam, Manipur, Meghalya, Mizoram, Nagaland, Sikkim, Tripura. For the purpose of this thesis, this last series of states will be indirectly included in the 'Southern model'. Close to the southern patterns are the states included in the eastern zone of Bihar, Orissa and West Bengal (Sen et al. 1997). Finally, Maharashtra and Gujarat are part of the Western zone of India (Sen et al. 1997).

[11] In spite of the fact that dowry is an illegal practice according to the *Dowry Prohibition Act* (1961).

hand, it has a transitional position between North and South in terms of literacy rates,[12] fertility rates,[13] sex ratio[14] and kinship organization.[15]

The economists Jean Drèze and Amartya Sen (1997) showed how socio-economic changes affect rural women of North and South India in different ways. Their comparative statistical analysis of gender inequality in selected states (particularly Uttar Pradesh and Kerala) is enlightening. However, this type of analysis cannot fully explain variation in the dependent variables. Indeed, Murthi, Guio and Drèze emphasize how important it is to take into account "differences in kinship systems, property rights, and related features of the economy and society", but they underline that there is insufficient data on these variations (Murthi et al. 1997: 387). I should add that there is also a lack of data on the construction of justice, rights and duties. The ways in which legal awareness is transmitted and transformed should also be considered as a pertinent variable.

---

[12] In India as a whole, 54% of females of the age of 7 and more are literate, and 76% of males. In Maharashtra, female literacy rate is 67% for females compared to a male rate of 86%. Yet Maharashtra lies between the Kerala rates (88% for female and 94% for male) and Uttar Pradesh (44% for female and 71% for male) (Drèze and Sen 2002).

[13] Between 1996 and 1998, the total fertility rate for India as a whole was 3.3 children per woman. In Maharashtra, this rate was 2.7 over the same period. Maharashtra's fertility rate lies between Kerala's 1.8 and Uttar Pradesh's 4.8 (Drèze and Sen 2002).

[14] Kerala is also exemplary in terms of infant mortality rate, which is of 11 deaths of children under the age of one per 1000 of live births compared to a national average of 60 deaths for the same amount of births, 76 deaths in Uttar Pradesh and 42 deaths in Maharashtra.

[15] Kinship patterns in Maharashtra are mostly related to North Indian culture, though the influence of southern cultures is significant in many respects (Carter 1974). Both Dravidian and Indo-Aryan kinship terminologies have influenced Marathi kinship (Bénéï 1996).

## 4. Daughters and Widows of Maharashtra: Shaping Identities in a Transitional Region

As several authors have noted, widowhood can lead to a family crisis that threatens the woman's economic security and survival (Agarwal 1994; Chen 1998, 2000; Chen and Drèze 1995). Various social factors influence the severity of the crisis, including age, education, employment, support by adult sons, support from the ex-husband's family, and support from the widow's natal family. How do Maharashtrian Hindu widows (and their children) cope with the loss of a senior male worker and property owner? How, and to what extent, do they take advantage of available legal reforms? Chen's recent book provides a cross-regional perspective on widowhood in seven Indian states (Chen 2000). However, Central and Western India are omitted, thus leaving a gap in the study of widows and property rights in the transitional zone between North and South.

Overall, the status of widows in Maharashtra is changing, as more alternatives to their state of dependency emerge. Recent local case studies in rural areas discuss the tremendous diversity in the experiences women have and demonstrate that women are not the sole victims when they are widowed (Jeffery et al. 1989, 1996; Raheja and Gold 1994). In fact, the loss of a senior male may provoke a family crisis that affects men, as well as women, and the impact on each family member varies according to their sex, age, economic situation, and status in the family and the village. However, it is clearly demonstrated in the literature that widows are more vulnerable than widowers.

Though many widows face major difficulties, some are helped by their natal or affinal families. Furthermore, a growing number of women in Maharashtra are gaining economic independence via increased access to education and employment. Widows' life experiences and inheritance practices can be better understood by reviewing the ideologies and the social expectations linked with womanhood and widowhood. As will be seen, certain beliefs and local practices associated with womanhood in Maharashtra affect the chances that daughters and widows will set out to claim their rights.

In nineteenth-century Bombay, the ideal wife or *pativrata* was defined as "the devoted wife whose entire existence is dedicated to her husband" (Leslie 1989: 1). This is a wife whose 'only duty' and 'main purpose in life' was service to her husband (Kapadia 1968: 169). The stereotype was long-lived. It is found in early

*Puranic* texts and the laws of Manu and Kautilya's *Arthashastra,* as well as in subsequent Hindu commentaries such as the *Stridharmapaddhati* written by the Brahman author Tryambaka. The influence of the latter persisted in the legal cases of the early nineteenth century. As pointed out by Sir Gooroodass Banerjee in his Tagore Law Lectures of 1878, early nineteenth century case precedents reaffirmed the applicability of Hindu Law on the position that "a woman's husband is like unto her god, and she must remain obedient to his orders and conform to his will" (Banerjee 1915: 119-120). It is true that the husband was directed to 'honour the wife' but as Banerjee pointed out, "[n]o system of law has ever surpassed our own in enjoining on the wife the duty of obedience to the husband and veneration for his person" (Banerjee 1915: 120). The ideal of *pativrata* still influences women's lives, as clearly demonstrated when we look at widows' experiences in Bheema.

Among Hindus, the ideology of widowhood includes references to some forms of *suttee,*[16] asceticism, and sexual control. None of the respondents I spoke with could remember hearing about cases of *suttee*, not even during their grandmothers' or great-grandmothers' time, although they knew that this practice used to be current in North India. Some women mentioned instances of widows having their heads shaved, but these cases occurred over 40 years ago and mostly among Marathas. The practice does not take place nowadays.

Nowadays widows wear colourful bangles but other jewellery is rare. *Mangalsutra*[17] is removed and burned with the husband's body, after which the widow will wear a simpler necklace, which is not made of gold. The *kumkum*[18] (married women's red dot on the forehead) is replaced by a black dot. I did not observe any widows wearing white saris in Bheema or in any other rural areas of Pune district, unlike other parts of India. On the other hand, widows' saris are often pale-coloured and of lesser quality than other women's saris.

Women from the village I studied were all of the opinion that the impact of the loss of a husband depends on the 'widow's behaviour'. When I asked what they meant by that it was difficult to obtain clear answers, but they did say that a widow

---

[16] *Suttee* refers to the immolation of the widow upon her husband's funeral pyre.

[17] A woman's bridal necklace made of black pearls with two ornaments and five gold beads.

[18] The red dot on the forehead worn by a married woman.

should be 'nice' to people in the community and should maintain a good reputation. Having observed the fragility of women's status, and their vulnerability to gossip, we can infer from these comments that the widow should not have 'affairs' (in the sense of love affairs) with men. Hence, fancy saris can be considered to be too attractive for a widow. Her appearance should be simple, and her sexuality should be constrained. Although the remarriage of widows may be acceptable in lower castes, this is a forbidden practice in the higher castes, especially among Marathas and Brahmins. Many widows said that, even if it was possible, they would not remarry. But many admitted that it was more difficult for a young woman to remain a widow because it would be harder for her to support herself and her young children.[19]

Overall, while widows' lives have to be simple and discreet (and have to be seen to be so), they do not fit the image of strict social exclusion mostly associated with a northern pattern. In Maharashtra, widows seem to be better off than in other regions, although they are excluded from rituals and festivals, which results in sadness. These observations are quite apart from the personal grief that women feel from losing someone with whom they have shared their life. The importance of a husband in a woman's life is underlined through the observance of certain festivals and fasts dedicated to the husband's health and long life. Widows who have lost their husbands recently express insecurity and loneliness.

The predicaments of widows do not feature in widowers' lives. Apart from potential sadness, widowers continue their lives without having to show any external signs of their loss and it is socially acceptable for them to remarry. Also during marriage, husbands are not pressured to follow any rituals or fasts centered on the well-being of their wives.

Overall, women who lost their husbands more than fifteen years ago tend to have suffered more than those who were widowed more recently. Respondents typically explained this by saying that social expectations of widows were different – that is, stricter – fifteen years ago or more. Social isolation was greater because the belief that widows were inauspicious was more widely held by family and community members, especially among the Maratha and the Brahmin castes.

---

[19] According to the *Hindu Widows Remarriage Act* (1983), the widows can legally remarry.

The identity of a woman continues to be largely defined according to her marriage and to the network of her husband. In spite of the increased social mobility of widows in Bheema, which reflects changes in the overall situation of women, they still do not claim their inheritance rights.

## 5. Inheritance Practices in Bheema

When I asked widows whether they had access to their husband's property, the majority of them answered that they had a right to it after his death. However, the respondents never mentioned the HSA, leading to the inference that they are not aware of this specific law. The actual understanding of inheritance rights is vague and varies considerably. For example, the majority of women believe that it is necessary to go to court in order to obtain a share. Also, it was never mentioned that the law divided the property between the widows and the children (sons and daughters). No women mentioned that a will could take precedence over the law and therefore deprive a widow of her codified rights (or accord her additional ones).

Overall, contrary to widespread belief, women in rural areas do know that they are entitled to some rights as widows. When asked how they had learned of the law, two answers came through clearly, either from television or by word of mouth from other villagers, family members and neighbours. No one mentioned that they had learned their rights in school. Whether or not this awareness is sufficient to encourage them to claim their rights is a more subtle issue. The mere knowledge of the existence of rights does not ensure access to property. Therefore, like in the past, the widows from rural areas seldom have any rights in land or other forms of property. In order to understand this continuity of practice it is necessary to see the law not as a set of fixed rules and institutions, but as a space of social interactions (Moore 1978).

When I asked Sunita, a married woman, about her access to property, she explained that her husband provided her with everything she needed. If she asked her brothers to give her a legal share in familial property, then they would be very unhappy. Now, she has the love of her brothers and they never forget to give her saris at various festivals, which is very meaningful to women. Sunita also mentioned that she is welcomed in the homes of her brothers when she visits them periodically. Village exogamy applies in most arranged marriages and implies that after marriage the bride moves into her husband's pre-existing household. In

Sunita's case, it was approximately 35 km from her natal village. Hence her comment: "What would I do with that land? Nothing! It is in another village and I will lose the love of my brothers!"

Her spontaneous reaction exemplifies the feedback of the women interviewed in the village, and also represents the practices related to legal claims. In general, to go to the police or court is not well regarded by women or men. Claiming inheritance rights to her deceased husband's property also shames the widow and her natal family. Some men told me that before going to the court, the brothers of a widow try to solve the matter directly with the other family. Men also mentioned that it is their duty to help their sister when she becomes a widow. However, many widows, especially the elder ones, have lost contact with their brothers or receive little help from them in practice. Hence, many widows live with both economic and emotional insecurities.

Women utilized social factors to explain why they did not, or would not, claim their rights. As a young female pointed out, "it is not good to create conflict with the parents-in-law. We have to keep quiet for the sake of our children". This reasoning is also found among the widows who do not continue to stay with their in-laws after the death of their husbands, even though they have been practically abandoned by the families of their husbands.

Another problem is that if a young widow becomes the owner of some property, it would modify the power relationship with her own mother-in-law who may not have an official property title. A change in the generational hierarchy of rural joint families may also lead to various social tensions. In addition, if a widow has adult sons, then there is little possibility that she will go to court to claim a share in her deceased husband's property which may instead go against her own son's interests.

As a sister, a woman is very uncomfortable in claiming her rights to a share of the father's property. Women who have already received some goods from their parents are reluctant to claim more from their familial property because they feel their parents and brothers already spent so much on their marriage and their dowry. An important problem for a widow, if her in-laws abandoned her, is to recover her *hunda* (dowry). They also find it very intimidating to ask for something from their in-laws, even their own saris, jewels and so on. In fact, women often do not know exactly what their *kunda* consisted of.

Women do not see the advantages of claiming their inheritance rights. If they claim their inheritance, they risk disrupting their security network along with jeopardizing the reputation of their family. For example, if a young married girl loses her husband and takes the initiative to consult a lawyer, to obtain her share in his property, her action will be very negatively perceived by her own natal family. First of all, she will be perceived as rebellious and undisciplined because she did not ask her natal kin if she should take legal action. However, if she had done so, they would probably have refused to go to court. Instead, her brothers (if she had any) would have tried to negotiate with her in-laws to ensure that she continued to be treated well despite losing her husband. Secondly, her independent initiative would diminish the possibility her unmarried brothers and sisters would have in finding suitable partners to marry, because a bad reputation is gained by the parents of a vindictive widow.

If a woman finally brings her case to court, it is not often an individual decision, but instead it will be a familial one. Both financial and psychological support from the brothers, and some members of the extended family, is necessary in most cases to confront the legal system. Changes in individual rights are difficult to implement in a society where the actions of one person are deeply embedded in a kinship network.

## 6. Going to Court: A Learning Process of Personality Building

In a context of legal pluralism, people will use various forums of justice depending on power and social relationships between the different claimants.

> Which specific repertoire, in which specific case, people will
> orient themselves to, will mostly be a matter of expediency, of
> local knowledge, perceived contexts of interaction, and power
> relations (Spiertz 2000: 191).

At this point, before looking at the state court system, it is pertinent to explore the alternatives to filing a lawsuit. Nowadays, caste *panchayat* (caste council, led by the elders of the caste) in Pune and its region are not very active, except in some tribal communities. However, even before the creation of a national court system, caste *panchayat* did not really deal with 'women's issues' except in cases where a property claim created a dispute between two families.

Women may go to a women's organization to obtain advice or deal with the conflict through mediation. In the Pune district, such organizations are concentrated in the city of Pune and its immediate surrounding areas. But even where organizations or social workers are present in the community, widows seldom seek their advice. Firstly, women are not always aware of the presence of these organizations. Secondly, as described above, widows seldom claim their general rights for all types of socio-economic reasons that also render them an underprivileged part of society. If they do not go to Court, it is unlikely that they will seek help from another organization, although they may approach them to find sources of financial aid in order to ensure the education of their children.

There are few institutions and organizations that offer alternatives for conflict resolution. We have seen why and how women tend to avoid conflicts. The process of claiming her rights implies that a woman will, to some extent, adopt a deviant behavior by defying the norms defining womanhood. Once in the realm of the state legal system, and on the margins of its bureaucracy, women – and men – have to modify the way they present and interpret their life experiences to 'fit' within the parameters of the legal culture of a particular court. Both the individual's level of education and the quality of communication between them and their lawyer play a vital role in the extent to which the claimant will shape his or her personality in order to achieve the status and identity recognized – and hence heard – by the legal system.

## 6.1 The Role of Education

Women's perception of the role of law does not imply that they are against change. In fact, women and men in the village are proud to talk about the improved position of women in the community, especially concerning their levels of education. According to the economists Jean Drèze and Amartya Sen, the role of education (along with health care) in India is crucial in provoking social changes, often more than legislative reforms (Drèze & Sen 2002).

As mentioned earlier, schooling has an unclear influence on legal awareness. Yet education has a positive impact on the ability to fill out official forms and to navigate through the bureaucracy. Moreover, as can be observed in the Pune District Court and Pune Family Court, education provides parties to a case with many tools necessary to understand and negotiate within the processes taking place within these tribunals. Ethnographic research conducted in the United States by

Conley and O'Barr (1998) underlines that the power of law is embedded in judicial language. "Law is a language, and it is through this language that the macro-dynamics of law's power play themselves out" (O'Barr 1998: 112. See also Mertz 1994). For example, people who speak assertively are more likely to be believed by the courts than people who speak deferentially (O'Barr 1982).[20] The *rule-oriented* claimants, compared to *relational-oriented* claimants, are favoured by judges of small claims courts in the United States because the language they use is better understood by the courts (Conley & O'Barr 1990: 58-59).[21]

For various reasons, it is not easy for women to be 'rule-oriented'. When they speak in front of a judge, at the Family Court or District Court, these women are often speaking in public for the first time, as also are many men. Not only is speaking in public an intrinsically intimidating experience, but the fact that women and men have to speak about their home life and their relationships with other household members can be demeaning.

The embarrassment may also lie in the fact that the hearings take place in both Marathi and English. The judge 'repeats' in English the 'statements' of the parties to the case and the witnesses, statements that were in Marathi. This is necessary so that the clerk can transcribe simultaneously the 'facts' in English for the court records. Such a translation is not necessarily precise and includes interpretations of the facts by the judge, in addition to the transformations of meanings due to the normal process of translation. The construction of narratives by disputants, the community and the court is an integral part of the disputing process (Just 1991), and these elements should be taken into account while studying access to justice. Consequently, education in English provides the claimants with additional means to be assertive and increase their control over the legal process.

In Pune district, like elsewhere in India education is not the only social factor influencing the relationship of women with the legal system. Yet, it is certainly an important element in the process of reshaping an identity that will fit the requirements of the state legal system and that will facilitate the control over

---

[20] This study was an interdisciplinary work: it combined anthropology, linguistics, social psychology and law.

[21] Claims courts were chosen as a site of study because these courts offer a legal environment in which judges invited the litigants to tell their story open-endedly, unlike in formal courtrooms.

resources. Ownership is not only an official title, it is an "umbrella concept" (F. and K. von Benda Beckmann and Spiertz 1996) which includes various types of rights, mainly the right to use a resource and the decision-making rights to regulate and control its use (F. and K. von Benda Beckmann and Spiertz 1997). Hence, to acquire and maintain property rights, the claimant should acquire a powerful personality that will be recognized by the community, as well as the court.

### 6.2 Relationships with a lawyer, and with the bureaucracy

In Family and District Courts the paperwork is in English. Therefore the claimants have to sign documents that they cannot understand. Hence, they have to rely completely on their lawyers, or on the judge, if they do not have a lawyer. Also, all the paperwork has to be completed by a legal professional, a lawyer, since the jargon of the legal system is very difficult for a layperson to understand.

It is also important that the lawyer prepares the client for her court appearance. The court is an official setting that can be intimidating. The claimant has to feel confident enough to listen carefully to what the judge or other lawyers are asking and to answer in a coherent manner. One requirement of the court discourse is that the witness should provide a chronological account of her story. To increase the chance to be well perceived, listened to and understood by the judge, a good lawyer will help the client in organizing the facts. A good level of communication between the lawyer and the client improves the client's chances of winning the case despite of the intricacies of the legal system.

The dense bureaucracy of the legal system and the governmental apparatus partly explains why access to justice is limited for widows. During my observation of court proceedings in the District Court of Pune, I realized that gaining access to property is often a highly technical procedure. For example, in order to obtain this right she has to produce her husband's death certificate. The ease with which the widow will be able to obtain the desired certificate seems to vary at random. Firstly, it is not always easy for a widow to go to the *gram panchayat*, or governmental offices, by herself. For most women, the paperwork that follows the death of their husbands will be the first administrative work that they have ever had to tackle on their own. Ration cards, caste certificates and birth certificates are almost always not kept in the hands of the woman, but rather by her father or, after marriage, by her husband. Even women who are breadwinners are not necessarily familiar with administrative work and negotiating with governmental agencies. The intricacies of governmental administration also transform the task of finding a simple piece of information into a real challenge, which can be very discouraging for someone who is unfamiliar with such procedures. Widows often told me of their concern and despair regarding administrative procedures. Indeed, their frustration is such that it is not uncommon to find widows who have given up pursuing access to their husband's pension, widow's pension, or other type of property to which they have a right.

In other cases, the widow has to go to court to obtain her husband's death certificate. For example, even in a case of intestate succession where the right of the widow is not disputed by the in-laws, the Government office may need the certificate to give the inheritance to the widow or one of her children. Then, what seems to be a pure formality can become a long judicial procedure, since it can easily take four or five years for a widow to obtain such a death certificate. During that time, she and her children are deprived of a source of income and a better social status.

Contrary to the official law, marriages are almost never registered, so it is very hard to prove officially that one is married. Clearly, if it is difficult to prove that someone was your husband, it will be even harder to claim rights to his property. Wedding photos and invitations often constitute good evidence that the wedding occurred, but these can be produced only if they are in the hands of the widow.

The costs associated with heavy bureaucracy are also important factors in influencing people's access to justice. Since the mid-1990s, women litigants in Maharashtra have been exempt from court fees in cases relating to maintenance, property, violence, and divorce. Still, the cost for lawyers' services can be very high. In one case, a widow claimed compensation for her husband's fatal accident but had no money left to claim her share in his property. Also, many women are not aware that they may have access to a government lawyer through legal aid. Lengthy procedures are also sources of discouragement from going to court or pursuing the legal matter to the end. Delays caused by numerous procedures also have the effect of further increasing the costs of the access to justice.

## Conclusion: Fighting for Property Rights: the Challenge of Acquiring a New Self

The long debate over personal laws led Indian legislators in the 1950s to choose a new 'social order'. In the process they created possible social disruption or 'social disorder', through a revision of the ideal of the Hindu joint household and the place of women and men within this model. If they follow this legislation, every household member has to reshape their parameters of identity, which leads them to appropriate a new sense of self.

In a transitional context of legal pluralism and rapid socio-economic change, before shopping for forums of justice (K. von Benda-Beckmann 1984), women will first – and not necessarily consciously – shop for 'avoidance of conflict forums'. In that space of conflict-avoidance, women, along with men, can reshape their sense of identity by balancing their constellation of rights and duties and renegotiating a meaning of justice.

Disputes over property are shaped and solved by various perceptions of women's rights, along with ideals of gender relationships and inter-generational organization. Legal anthropology provides a useful framework in which to understand the interplay of various concepts of rights and duties, within a context of legal pluralism. Legal anthropology also contributes to research on women's relationship to the legal system by focusing on the cultural analysis of

> the ways legal institutions and actors create meanings, the impact
> of these meanings on surrounding social relationships, and the
> effect of the cultural framework on the nature of legal procedures
> themselves (Engle Merry 1992: 360).

In spite of progressive legal initiatives in Maharashtra, women in Bheema do not see the advantages of claiming their inheritance rights. For, if they claim their inheritance, they risk disrupting their security network. Yet, since Independence, the social changes that have occurred in Bheema for both men and women, including widows, suggest that legal reforms concerning property rights may eventually be utilized by the population. Over recent decades the steady increase in literacy rates for men and women, the larger acceptance of female education in the formal and informal sectors, and the better community acceptance of women going outside the village for education and jobs indicate a deep movement towards social changes leading to larger gender equality. Those factors in the long term reduce the negative impacts of social indicators associated with the North (such as the prevalence of patrilocality and patrilineal inheritance practices). In Bheema, and Maharashtra, positive effects of education are already found in the fact that widowhood is less difficult among Hindu communities of Maharashtra than in the North. Schooling and a popular education movement have been crucial factors leading to, on the one hand, the reduction of biases concerning lower castes and widowhood and, on the other hand, to the slight but persistent increase in job opportunities for women.

If the Indian government really wishes to implement the HAS, legal literacy programs are necessary to educate the population on the benefits of women's access to property rights for the whole society. Moreover, the State must encourage local initiatives that aim to support communities as they face changes brought about by the reallocation of land and other forms of property.

# References

AGARWAL, Bina
1994    *A Field of One's Own: Gender and Land Rights in South Asia.*
        Cambridge: Cambridge University Press.
AGNES, Flavia
1999    *Law and Gender Inequality. The Politics of Women's Rights in India.*
        New Delhi: Oxford University Press.
ATTWOOD, D.W.
1995    'Inequality among Brothers and Sisters.' Working Papers, Centre for
        Society, Technology and Development, McGill University
n.d.    'Inequality among Brothers and Sisters, Part 1: Brothers.'
BANERJEE, Gooroodass
1915    *The Hindu Law of Marriage and Stridhana (Being the Tagore Law
        Lectures for 1878).* Calcutta: S.K. Lahiri.
BASU, Srimati
1999    *She Comes to Take her Rights.* New York: SUNY Press.
BENDA-BECKMANN, Keebet von
1984    *The Broken Staircase to Consensus: Village Justice and State Courts in
        Manangkabau.* Dordrecht, The Netherlands: Foris.

BENDA-BECKMANN, Franz von, Keebet von BENDA-BECKMANN and H.L. Joep SPIERTZ

1996    'Water Rights and Water Policy.' Pp. 77-100 in H.L. Joep Spiertz and Melanie G. Wiber (eds.), *The Role of Law in Natural Resource Management*, The Hague, The Netherlands: VUGA.

1997    'Local Law and Customary Practices in the Study of Water Rights.' Pp. 221-242 in Rajendra Pradhan, Franz von Benda-Beckmann, Keebet von Benda-Beckmann, H.L.Joep Spiertz, Shantam S. Khadka and K. Azharul Haq (eds.), *Water Rights, Conflict and Policy*, Colombo: IIMI.

BÉNÉÏ, Véronique

1996    *La dot en Inde: un fléau social?* Paris: Karthala.

BÉTEILLE, André

1986    'Individualism and Equality.' *Current Anthropology* 27: 121-134.

CALDWELL, John C., P.H. REDDY and Pat CALDWELL

1988.   *The Causes of Demographic Change: Experimental Research in South India.* Madison: University of Wisconsin Press.

CARTER, Anthony

1974    'A comparative analysis of systems of kinship and marriage in South Asia.' *Proceedings of the Royal Anthropological Institute of Great Britain and Ireland*: 29-54.

CHEN, Martha (ed.)

1998    *Widows in India: Social Neglect and Public Action.* New Delhi: Sage.

2000    *Perpetual Mourning: Widowhood in Rural India.* Oxford: Oxford University Press.

CHEN, Martha and Jean DRÈZE

1995    'Recent research on widows in India.' *Economic and Political Weekly*, 30 September.

CONLEY, James M. and William M. O'Barr

1990    *Rules versus Relationships. The Ethnography of Legal Discourse.* Chicago: University of Chicago Press.

1998    *Just Words: Law, Language, and Power (Language & Legal Discourse).* Chicago: Chicago University Press.

DANDEKAR, Hemalata C.

1986    *Men to Bombay, Women at Home: Urban Influence on Sugaon Village, Deccan Maharashtra, India, 1942-1982.* University of Michigan Papers of South & Southeast Asia.

DRÈZE, Jean and Amartya SEN

1997    *Indian Development: Selected Regional Perspectives.* Delhi: Oxford University Press.

2002    *India: Development and Participation.*New Delhi: Oxford University Press.

DYSON, Tim and Mick MOORE

1983    'On kinship, structure, female autonomy, and demographic behavior in India.' *Population and Development Review*, 9: 35-60.

EPSTEIN, T. Scarlett

1973. *South India: Yesterday, Today and Tomorrow (Mysore Villages Revisited).* London: Macmillan.

GoM (Government of Maharashtra)

1994    *Policy For Women.*

GRIFFITHS, Anne

2002    'Doing ethnography: living law, life histories, and narratives from Botswana.' In June Starr & Mark Goodale (eds.), *Practicing Ethnography in Law. New Dialogues, Enduring Methods*, New York: Palgrave Macmillan.

JEFFERY, Patricia, Roger JEFFERY and Andrew LYON

1989    *Labour Pains and Labour Power: Women and Child-Bearing in India.* London: Zed Books Ltd.

JEFFERY, Patricia and Roger JEFFERY

1996    *Don't Marry Me to a Plowman! Women's Everyday Lives in Rural North India.* Boulder: Westview Press.

1997    *Population, Gender and Politics:Demographic Change in Rural North India.* Cambridge University Press.

JUST, Peter

1991    'Conflict resolution and moral community among the Dou Donggo.' In Kevin Avruch, Peter W. Black and Joseph A. Scimecca (eds.), *Conflict Resolution: Cross-cultural Perspective.* New York: Greenwood University Press.

KAPADIA, Kanaiyalal M.

1966    *Marriage and Family in India.* London: Oxford University Press.

LESLIE, Joanne

1989.    'Women's work and child nutrition in the third world.' In *Women, Work and Child Welfare in the Third World.* Colorado: Westview Press.

MACLACHLAN, Morgan

1993    'Working mothers and bachelor farmers: an investigation of relationships between female farm labour participation and juvenile sex ratios in rural India.' *Contemporary South Asia* 2: 5-21.

MERRY, Sally Engle

1992    'Anthropology, law and transnational processes.' *Annual Review of Anthropology* 21: 357-379.

MERTZ, Elizabeth
1994    'Legal language: pragmatics, poetics, and social power.' *Annual Review of Anthropology* 23: 435-455.
MILLER, Barbara D.
1981    *The Endangered Sex: Neglect of Female Children in Rural North India.* New-York: Cornell University Press.
MINTURN, Leigh
1993    *Sita's Daughters: Coming Out of Purdah.* New York: Oxford University Press.
MOORE, Sally Falk
1978    *Law as Process. An Anthropological Approach.* London: Routledge.
MURTHI, Martha, Anne-Catherine GUIO and Jean DRÈZE
1997    'Mortality, fertility and gender bias in India: a district-level analysis.' Pp. 357-405 in Amartya. Sen and Jean Drèze (eds.), *Indian Development: Selected Regional Perspectives.* Delhi: Oxford University Press.
O'BARR, William M.
1982    *Linguistic Evidence: Language, Power and Strategy in the Courtroom.* New York: Academic Press.
1998    'Combining approaches: some reflections on two decades of collaborative research.' *PoLAR* 22: 110-114.
RAHEJA, Gloria.G. and Ann G. GOLD
1994    *Listen to the Heron's Words.* Los Angeles: University of California Press.
SHAH, A.M.
1974    *The Household Dimension of the Family in India.* Berkeley: University of California Press
1988    'The phase of dispersal in the Indian family process." *Sociological Bulletin* 37: 33-47.
SHARMA, Ursula
1980    *Women, Work, and Property in North-West India.* London: Tavistock.
SPIERTZ, H.L. Joep
2000    'Water rights and legal pluralism: some basics of a legal anthropological approach." Pp. 162-199 in Bryan R. Bruns and Ruth S. Meinzen-Dick (eds.), *Negotiating Water Rights*, London: Intermediate Technology Publications.
WADLEY, S.Susan
1994    *Struggling with Destiny in Karimpur, 1925-1984.* Berkeley: University of California Press.

# WHEN LEGAL PROCEDURALISM CONFUSES THE VALUES OF LEADERSHIP: 'OFFICIAL' AND 'UNOFFICIAL' LAW IN A TLINGIT COMMUNITY

Kathryn Fulton

## Introduction

Social systems are fundamentally political in character, so they are always vulnerable to those forces that are excluded in the process of political formation (Laclau 1990: 31-36). Such is the case in a community that I will call Keex' Kwaan, Alaska. Keex' Kwaan is a predominantly Native Tlingit community, where the political formations of a tribal corporation, an incorporated city and a tribal government were modeled after Euro-American law and business standards. Under Euro-American procedural models of decision-making, the Tlingit 'unofficial' law priorities of community consensus were systematically weakened and even excluded. One result is a sense of mistrust and pessimism in Keex' Kwaan toward local leadership and governing entities. This sense of political negativity is a major hurdle for local problem-solving during a time of increasing economic crisis. Based on ethnographic fieldwork, this paper addresses the circumstances through which Euro-American legal processes have been superimposed on Tlingit social resources for managing conflict and the 'unofficial' laws of leadership in the village. Local tension results from trying to live within incompatible values. Another consequence is a division of leadership, restricting the ability of the city, the tribe and the tribal corporation to cooperate. Over time, division of leadership without community-wide consensus building has contributed to intrinsic skepticism of most representatives elected or hired into leadership positions.

A basic proposition in discourse theory is that antagonisms, such as those in Keex' Kwaan, show the points where identity is no longer fixed in a specific system, but contested by forces that stand outside, or at the very limit, of that order (Norval 1997). Another similar premise of discourse theory is that antagonisms reveal limit points in society through which social meaning is contested and which cannot be stabilized without change (Howarth and Stavrakakis 2000: 9). In Keex' Kwaan, 'unofficial' Tlingit law has been contested by outside forces for at least 15 decades, but contestation has accelerated in the past three decades. In the first part of the 20th century Euro-American legal procedures, such as elections and Roberts Rules of Order, were a minimal part of people's daily lives. Examples included city government business or the Alaska Native Brotherhood and Sisterhood. In the 1970s and 1980s, when Keex' Kwaan Tlingits became shareholders in a corporation that had jurisdiction over Keex' Kwaan Tribal Land, participation in Euro-American legal procedures affected everyone in the community more deeply. By the later part of the 1980s some groups began to openly question outside legal and economic forces and values. In the 1990s and now in 2005, revitalization of Tlingit laws and values grows stronger. 'Unofficial' Tlingit laws 'stand outside or at the very limit' of the state and US federal legal complex, but they continue to be important in day to day local interpersonal relationships.

In Keex' Kwaan, antagonisms and tensions over power and leadership decidedly do reveal the limit points through which social meaning is contested. Law-making through boards and councils - made up of people elected to represent the electorate - is a legislative process that is performed in problematic contrast to 'unofficial' values such as family loyalty, reciprocity and elder leadership. Official public meetings that are overseen by a group of elected representatives fail to provide an adequate forum for the 'unofficial' value of community-wide consensus building: reorganization of Keex' Kwaan law-making through boards and councils could be considered a type of coercive assimilation. Gaventa (1982) discussed one dimension of coercive social power called 'process power'. Process power "shapes the playing field" (Docherty 2004: 865). For this paper I extend the concept of coercive process power to include the Euro-American legal standards through which all United States' incorporated cities and business corporations must conduct their legal functions. I include in my description of coercive process power the US legal standards through which participants are included or excluded from boards and councils based upon appointments and elections. Some legislators work under the assumption that such formal, bureaucratic proceduralism is unavoidable within the contemporary US because the country as a whole lacks a dominant identity. For Keex' Kwaan Tlingits, however, Euro-American proceduralism contributes to a current economic crisis and local political polarization that makes economic problem-solving difficult. In the case of Keex' Kwaan, the legal procedures of decision-making through boards and councils, which has been imposed through relatively inflexible Euro-American principles of incorporation, can be seen as a type of 'process power'.

Public council and board meetings are the standard legal Euro-American solution to constituent participation. In Keex' Kwaan a different kind of community meeting would augment local empowerment. A state and federal encouragement of legal pluralism within decision-making procedures would assist Keex' Kwaan in formation of cooperative and consensual leadership. Changes in public decision-making processes could be a means to build respect for leadership into Keex' Kwaan's political situation. Without respect for leadership, the community lacks collective power for finding social and economic solutions.

## The Circumstances and History of Keex' Kwaan

To begin, Keex' Kwaan is a tribal Tlingit village. Most of Keex' Kwaan's surroundings are national forest land, part of the Tongass National Forest. The population, until recently, was approximately 650 people. Since December 2003 at least 200 people have moved to seek employment. More are planning to leave if they can find jobs elsewhere and accumulate enough money to move. Keex' Kwaan's fish processing plant closed in 2004, partly because of the low price which wild fish commands now that farmed Atlantic salmon dominates the world market. The same year, 2004, marked the end of logging in Keex' Kwaan and the Keex' Kwaan Tribal Corporation is negotiating possible bankruptcy, or what is called 'financial reorganization'. In the summer months of 2004 I noted a greater emphasis on subsistence fishing, hunting and berry picking, reminiscent of times past.

Until the 1970s Keex' Kwaan people relied heavily on traditional and customary fishing, hunting and berry picking. Many worked at commercial fishing and processing. Changes in the emphasis on and availability of traditional and customary foods and changes in economic priorities are connected to the enactment of various state and federal laws, including the 1971 Alaska Native Claims Settlement Act (ANCSA). Instead of designating land within an Indian reservation system, the act required Keex' Kwaan Tlingits to form the Keex' Kwaan Tribal Corporation (not its real name) under the legal umbrella of a regional corporation.

Native corporations were required to make a profit from the lands allotted through the settlement. Through ANCSA corporation management, the land around Keex' Kwaan has been logged so extensively that the only trees left to cut are protecting one third of the community watershed. (In 2005 a desperate city council voted to allow additional logging in the watershed.) Much of the profit that resulted from logging was distributed to native shareholders. Much of the money was lost through poor management and internal and external corruption, according to local narrative. I was informed that fewer than 40% of voting corporate shareholders live in Keex' Kwaan.

Donald Mitchell (1997) wrote that ANCSA was a move that the US Congress made to economically assimilate Alaska Natives and, inadvertently, to weaken their traditional cultures. To inquire whether ANCSA was good or bad is to ask whether or not economic assimilation through corporations benefited Alaska Natives in ways that exceeded the cost of cultural disruptions.

For people in Keex' Kwaan, ANCSA is a factor in increasing polarization between those who are working to re-vitalize traditional community and environmental values and those who feel that environmentally concerned individuals are to blame for the loss of resource extraction jobs. People whose cash-economy livelihoods came from logging are concerned about the loss of forest extraction jobs, not just on tribal lands but in the Tongass National Forest in general. For their part, those concerned about older Tlingit values tell the following story.

In the 1980s the local and regional ANCSA corporations distributed dividends to their shareholders from the profits they made from logging and other enterprises. Paradoxically, as corporation checks for thousands of dollars began to appear in people's mailboxes, the suicide rate in Keex' Kwaan grew to be the highest in the nation. Social program experts came to help with the increasing drug, violence and suicide problems. Economic experts came to help the tribal corporation remain lucrative. The experts came and went and little changed. Local groups decided they needed to take action themselves. They needed to use their sovereign powers as a tribe to re-vitalize the traditional values of community, reciprocity and environmental responsibility. A group of people began to practice and implement their rights as an Indian Reorganization Act (IRA) tribe. Their tribal organization is the Organized Village of Keex' Kwaan (OVK, not its real name). Today OVK writes its own grants and administers, for Keex' Kwaan, the federal monies allotted to the tribe for social services, housing and health care. OVK is separate from the ANCSA Keex' Kwaan Tribal Corporation.

In 1993, the Clinton administration conferred on many Alaska tribes a sovereignty through which they would have 'government to government' relations with the US government. This action further empowered the local tribe in Keex' Kwaan to write grants and receive direct federal funding for the benefit of Keex' Kwaan natives. In 2003-2004 Senator Ted Stevens, R. Alaska, and others worked to rescind the status of Alaska tribes and to regionalize tribal health care, housing, courts, justice services and other programs for tribes. Stevens gave as his reasons administrative costs, efficiency, compliance, accountability, inequitable distribution of competitive grants and the problem of small or relocated tribes (Harrison 2003).

A third governing entity in Keex' Kwaan is the incorporated City of Keex' Kwaan. The city is responsible for Keex' Kwaan public works and local police services. Its main source of revenue is the community liquor store. Keex' Kwaan, in 1912, was the first Tlingit community to incorporate as a city. At that time the elders formally made the decision to abandon their Tlingit ways and join the 'white man's' governing system and world (Johnson 2001). The narrative about the 1912 decision was told to me often in Keex' Kwaan, but most often with a sense of regret. Traditionally, strict formal laws governed the relations between clans, but formal laws did not apply to the decision-making and internal affairs between individuals and houses (Worl 1998: 226). Everyday human relations and leadership, and the choosing of leaders as representatives in clan affairs were governed through 'unofficial' laws and values. After the US Navy bombed Keex' Kwaan villages in 1859, and after incorporation as a city, the formal clan laws fell away in Keex' Kwaan,. 'Unofficial' laws have endured and are still evident in day-to-day relationships and special events.


## Current Political Conditions and 'Unofficial' Laws in Keex' Kwaan

Throughout my fieldwork experience I have heard about and observed the 'spinning wheels' of leadership in the tribal corporation and the city government. Because the goals and purposes of the IRA tribe, the tribal corporation and the city are felt to be philosophically opposed, and because of family and clan loyalties that I will describe later in the paper, the three governing entities have resisted meeting and working together. Social and economic issues are decided separately within boards and councils rather than jointly in ways that take into consideration the interrelationship of local concerns. This polarization of leadership exemplifies the juxtaposition between Tlingit laws and 'official' laws and the legal entities formed around 'official' laws.

Based on fieldwork in Keex' Kwaan, I can identify several traditional values that are manifest in present day Keex' Kwaan 'unofficial' or community laws. I will discuss four and how they conflict with legal and economic expectations that originated outside of Keex' Kwaan. Formal and 'official' Euro-American laws have failed to transform Keex' Kwaan and many other native villages into fully economically 'assimilated' communities. I will describe some of the reactions of state and federal legislators to assimilation failures.

Presently Keex' Kwaan and some other tribes find solutions to many social problems through autonomy and a philosophy of 'self-determination'. Economic problems, entwined with other social problems, are more difficult to solve locally, partly because of the philosophical differences between ANCSA corporations which have jurisdiction over tribal lands, and other local groups. In the mean time, state lawmakers periodically propose that local governing forces be consolidated regionally. Federal legislators campaign for regionalization of tribal social programs. Consolidation and regionalization are likely to further disempower local leadership and increasingly disengage the decision-making process from 'unofficial' laws and values. The points I make in this paper show why creating new elected positions on regional boards and councils would constrict autonomy and 'self-determination' and further divide community leadership. Local, 'bottom up' cooperative problem-solving would likely become even more difficult than it is now.

Two sets of recent conversations in Keex' Kwaan exemplify how Tlingit laws influence leadership and cooperation issues. During the Dog Salmon Festival in July 2004 an elder pointed out a 'real' Tlingit chief among the dancers from Juneau. I asked him if anyone in Keex' Kwaan is considered a 'real' chief. He told me 'no,' but there are 'pretenders'. He said that when Keex' Kwaan people decided to give up their Tlingit ways in 1912, they gave up having chiefs. In other conversations he described the attributes of a Tlingit chief. First the chief needed to take care of and repair his house every year and there should be smoke coming out of his chimney. Second, his job was to respect the will of the people with humility and not for personal gain.

Chief, of course, is a Euro-American term with all its implied meanings. Even before 1912 there were no chiefs. "There were just men put forward by the clan to represent them and, by consensus put forward by the village, to represent them for a specific doing." There were specialists in every area of life from planting to warriors to medicines, and there were specialists for every community gathering. (Jackson 2005)

Several older people in Keex' Kwaan remember how leadership was practiced after 1912, when they were children. One woman described how people often solved community problems by calling a community meeting. Everyone in the village was invited and most people came and participated, she said. Family representatives had the opportunity to express how they saw issues and what they thought should be done. The respected elders/leaders made the final decisions, but their decisions were based upon community consensus and the will of the people. The elders' decisions were followed because within family groups and clans young people were educated to respect their elders.

Although Keex' Kwaan renounced its Tlingit ways in 1912, a study of the village shows that a decision to give up traditional laws does not make 'unofficial' laws disappear. They remain a part of behavioral expectations and they influence the ability of ANCSA corporation, tribal and city leaders to adhere to 'official' laws that are in conflict with local values.

Four Tlingit laws are considered in this paper:

1) The inter-relationship of respect for elders as leaders, belief in the importance of the will of the people, and belief in the importance of decision-making through consensus.
2) The importance of family loyalty, sharing, 'pride,' and particular reciprocity responsibilities between families, and, at special times, between clans and moieties.
3) The practice of helping those in need and assisting those who have experienced losses.
4) The values of respect for animals, plants, the earth and especially for traditional and customary foods. Such values are ideologically interwoven with the values of taking only what is needed from the environment and thanking the creatures, plants and landforms for their help and offerings.

The four 'unofficial' laws summarized here are ideals that people follow in varying degrees. Because remnants of these laws continue to influence Keex' Kwaan people, their lives are partially situated in the ideals of older resource distribution practices and social relationship expectations. Such Tlingit ideals and practices are often in contrast to the practices and expectations of the state and federal legislative, regulatory and enforcement system inherent in corporate businesses and government agencies.

As stated before, one result of living within and between local, Tlingit ideals and Euro-American capitalist ideals is that local leadership has been weakened. Community-wide meetings, where respected leaders/elders listened to everyone voice their concerns and ideas, rarely if ever occur now. Most community-wide gatherings now are funeral dinners, what are called 40-day dinners, and pay back dinners. Funeral dinners are well attended and their adherence to Tlingit protocol and the commonly understood distribution of labor between families, clans and moieties demonstrates that Keex' Kwaan people have maintained the organizational networks for consensual decision-making.

Presently political decisions are made through the elected officials of boards and councils in the tribe, the corporation and the city. Typically people are highly critical of those who serve on boards, councils and committees. The council and board members' motivations and rights to make decisions are questioned on a daily basis. People say that the representatives are almost always elected because they have big families who vote for them out of loyalty. Some people say that one large family runs the corporation, the city and the tribe. Others point out that a different large family runs each entity, but that they are intermarried. Leadership through respected elders still seems to be the decision-making ideal, even though such leadership is not officially practiced. Older people, as youngsters, were taught in living history the importance of respecting elders as leaders. Young people still learn the importance of respecting their elders. In the past, the respected leaders were elders who demonstrated through life that they were trustworthy, humble, good listeners, respectful to others, and generous with what they had. Now, in contrast, village people perceive that the elected leadership of their corporation and government entities is based upon familial loyalties and nepotism. Only a few elected leaders are considered elders in the Tlingit law sense.

The situation in Keex' Kwaan brings to mind Witteveen's (1999) observation that legislation is like a symphony. Just as there is a division of labor in a symphony between the musicians and the conductor, so also there is a division of labor in legislation between the lawmakers and the constituents.

To achieve the minimum acceptable results, the authority of the
conductor (law maker) must not be in doubt, and all the
musicians (constituents) must have more or less the same notions
of how to act as good musicians.

In Keex' Kwaan people may attempt to perform in at least two symphonies at the
same time. The result of attempting to adhere to two political and social value
systems is confusion and disillusionment. Village leadership authority is in doubt
partly because few leaders are elders in the ideal sense and partly because local
elected representatives make decisions without the consensus that comes from
more traditional community meetings and communication processes. Community
issues have been divided between the corporation, the city and the tribe. Most
people on the island agree that ANCSA exacerbated local divisions. Several tribal
and city representatives said that Keex' Kwaan could have been a place of
community cooperation without the corporation. The ANCSA corporation became
a wedge between them.

In August 2004 I began asking people which members of the community they
would respect as leaders. Some people could name one or two, who tended to be
elders. Some people were surprised at their own answers because they could not
name anyone. They said that most of the people they respected had died. Where
are the elders to replace the ones passed on, I asked? People have been asking that
question themselves for as long as I have been in Keex' Kwaan. There are older
people in the community, but most do not participate as teachers or leaders. People
told me the older people are staying quiet for a number of reasons. First, they are
of the generation that was sent off to boarding schools, or whose teachers in the
village punished them for speaking in Tlingit. They learned to be ashamed of
Tlingit ways of doing things. These parents and grandparents often wanted to
protect their children from experiencing the same pain in school and refused to
teach them about Tlingit culture and language. Many elders still see the end of
Tlingit culture and language as a way to save their children and grandchildren
from suffering. Second, many older people are of a generation that was caught up
in alcohol, drug abuse, violence and other destructive forms of behavior. Many
feel unworthy to be elders in the traditional sense. According to Tlingit law, an
elder is a leader because he or she is a living example of Tlingit values.

As mentioned before, a few people aspire to be non-elected leaders. Their attempts
at leadership are typically criticized, although their work is on the whole beneficial
to Keex' Kwaan people. I asked why these leaders are often, but not always

discussed without respect, and I was told, through stories, that they do not meet the behavioral criteria of a leader. People accuse such aspiring leaders of lacking humility. People assert that aspiring 'chiefs' are too concerned with their own notoriety. There is a sense that they often behave arrogantly and thus have lost the wisdom that their purpose is to serve. As one elder said, pride is important among Tlingit families, but there is a difference between 'pride' and being 'proud'. One man wants to be 'chief' of his clan in order 'to make decisions,' but an elder told me that such a desire is not a characteristic of a good leader. True leaders follow the will of the people after people have had a chance to express and discuss their feelings and ideas.

Related to Keex' Kwaan leadership disparity, other Tlingit laws often subvert and are subverted by the 'official' legal, decision-making standards of corporations and incorporation. They include the importance of family loyalty, sharing and 'pride'. Families reportedly elect their own members onto city, tribal and ANCSA corporation boards and councils. When people are in city, corporate or tribal positions, they are accused of hiring family members as employees because of family loyalties. The importance of helping those in need and those who have experienced loss of a loved one, a boat, a house or a job is another local law. Ideally what has been shared will be shared again. These local, 'unofficial' laws make collecting public utility bills and enforcing ordinances difficult for the city. Some people may owe $3,000 in water and sewer payments, but the city typically refrains from cutting their services out of respect for family and other relationships and out of humanistic respect for people's losses. Few people pay for keeping their boats at the boat harbor, for example. If police officers are members of local families, they often find that family and neighbor relationships inhibit equitable law enforcement.

Other Tlingit laws concerning respect for animals, plants and especially subsistence foods are difficult to maintain within the constructs of Euro-American corporate and incorporated legal and organizational patterns. Many Keex' Kwaan people say they still practice the rituals of thanks when they harvest salmon, trees and other resources. Related to the law of respect is the law that one should never take more than what one needs of a resource. This Tlingit law is one reason that many, but not all people in a predominantly Caucasian fishing community 45 air miles away often speak in critical tones about Keex' Kwaan. In the context of traditional Tlingit values they judge as hypocritical the tribal corporation's cutting of its entire forest holdings.

Keex' Kwaan narratives express concern about such contradictions. Villagers emphasize expectations that Tlingit people will practice local and traditional Tlingit laws concerning the environment, family and other relationships. At the same time people feel that they should be successful within the Euro-American corporate, economic, and legal complex. Outside narratives express the same expectations. Keex' Kwaan people feel a sense of embarrassment and loss because their ANCSA corporation failed within both Tlingit law and 'official' law parameters.

Prioritizing autonomy and self-governance, OVK, the IRA tribe, is closer than other Keex' Kwaan governing entities to accomplishing a philosophical and decision-making fit between Tlingit law expectations and the requirements of working within the state/federal legislative and economic legal system. The OVK staff successfully administers grants. It recently received an award from the Kennedy School of Government, Harvard University for its Circle Peacemaking efforts in suicide prevention, interventions for alcoholism and drug abuse, domestic violence, personal and cultural traumas, and restorative justice work. Through the Organized Village Circle Peacemaking, people have revived and practice Tlingit consensus-building. Keex' Kwaan has initiated a justice system that increasingly involves community members in identification and healing of problems. The tribe created a safe place for young people to gather and has been instrumental in restoring cultural pride and in teaching cultural values. As stated before, its successes may be recognized locally, but its leaders are often criticized. Local, 'unofficial' laws concerning elders, leadership, family, loyalty and 'pride' are some of the reasons that local people discuss with non-respect current and past tribal leadership. The village continues to experience high levels of unemployment, poverty and drug and alcohol abuse. Such problems are more difficult to solve with the legal and philosophical separation of tribe from city from ANCSA corporation.

When opportunities for cooperation present themselves, 'official' legal rules and laws often subvert attempts to solve problems through 'unofficial' local Tlingit laws. For example, the city has jurisdiction over the community fish hatchery. The tribal corporation owes the hatchery a substantial sum of money. The corporation is in the midst of possible bankruptcy (or 'financial reorganization'), so the mayor devised a plan to help the city and the corporation work together to prevent animosity and a lawsuit. A few years ago the mayor devised a similar and successful plan to help the city out of impending 'bankruptcy'. However, in the case of the corporation the lawyer representing the hatchery and the city told the mayor publicly that his suggestions, while they may have been good solutions, compromised the city's legal position. The mayor was told that he should have stayed quiet. In effect, the city could only come out ahead if it maintained a victim/perpetrator relationship with the tribal corporation. While the lawyer was probably correct, the example shows that 'official' legal processes often increase polarization between local governing entities, inhibit cooperative leadership, and intensify local mistrust of village leadership.

Bourdieu (1991: 250) theorized that when the political field is increasingly professionalized and when only a few people have power to speak on behalf of other groups, then leadership generates a culture of political practices from which ordinary people are excluded. Within such political systems certain types of knowledge are taken for granted. Certain subjects are never discussed and certain questions are never raised or answered. Ideally, within 'unofficial' Keex' Kwaan laws, people might have solved legal problems through internal conversations between families and clans. They might have participated in community-wide meetings where respected leaders listened and made decisions based upon the will of the people.

Now Keex' Kwaan is in economic crisis, and while the tribe and the city attempt to communicate, community wide meetings in the Tlingit law sense had yet to be organized by the time this paper was written. Jurisdiction over a community-wide meeting is problematic considering the competitiveness between the families that run the three governing entities and 'official' legal separation between the tribe, the corporation and the city. The tribal corporation, which controls most of Keex' Kwaan land, is uncommunicative. Its shareholders are uninformed about the reasons and circumstances of possible bankruptcy or "financial reorganization". The corporation's silence is an element of Euro-American legal practices, but it excludes community participation and problem solving.

## Conclusion: Assessment of Current Trends

The aim of this paper has been to outline how legal procedural law transforms Keex' Kwaan relationships in ways that divide families, neighbors and purposes. The limitations of Euro-American legal processes have inhibited Keex' Kwaan's ability to achieve consensus building. Keex' Kwaan's situation demonstrates how 'liberal law' in the Euro-American tradition, is "tendentiously assimilationist" (Tie 1999: 201). Presently Alaska state and federal legislative logic presumes that legal procedural law, based upon representation through elected boards and councils, is the best means for problem-solving and for resolving conflicts within all of its communities. Michael Walzer (1992) proposed that bureaucratic and legal proceduralism may be unavoidable within contemporary America because the nation-state lacks a dominant identity. In examining the Keex' Kwaan situation, Euro-American legal proceduralism has contributed to a loss of community and cultural identity. The Keex' Kwaan example demonstrates a need for legal process flexibility and pluralism and supports Warwick Tie's statement that within legal proceduralism "particular cultural identities ought to be recognized" (1999: 203). Formal procedural legal practices leave many Keex' Kwaan people out of the decision-making process.

A legal pluralism of decision-making processes could be successful in Keex' Kwaan. People demonstrate their capacity for working together and consensus-building through the growing influence of Circle Peacemaking and the community-wide cooperation evident in funeral dinners and other events. This capacity could be strengthened through stronger state and federal recognition of the value of legal pluralism within the legal processes that govern corporations and incorporated cities and tribes. Legal pluralism would involve increasing local legal autonomy and 'self-determination' so that Keex' Kwaan people could reconceptualize their legal decision-making processes in ways that strengthen local consensus and 'unofficial' local laws. Conversely, the diminution of autonomy and self-determination through regionalization of tribal services would counter day-to-day 'unofficial' law, knowledge and consensus-building efforts.

Instead of stressing cooperation from within, many state and federal legislators propose consolidation from without. Applicable to the situation is Weisbrod's statement that "the emphasis on the state is parallel to the historical tendency of American law toward centralization ... The master trend is 'to create one legal culture out of many; to reduce legal pluralism'" (Weisbrod 2002: 3, 4). Proposed legislation to require formation of borough governments in rural Alaska is an example. State laws require eventual state-wide borough formation, but it is important to note that such legislation occurred in the 1950s during a period when assimilation of Native Americans and others was considered a solution to their social and economic problems. Currently the state legislative focus on borough formation centers on regions that include more rural native villages than other southeast Alaska areas. Reasons given for proposed legislation include the 'necessity' to centralize local governments in order to facilitate more efficient taxation of resource extraction. Legislators who support centralization assert that taxation of resource extraction through boroughs will provide a better system for funding schools, roads and other services.

Other examples of attempts to further reduce local power through centralization include federal efforts toward regionalization of Alaska tribes. Senator Stevens stated in October 2003 that there are too many tribes in Alaska, and Alaska Native 'sovereignty' has become a threat to statehood. State and federal centralization and regionalization would effectively disempower the IRA tribe's social program efforts and its autonomy to make decisions about how federal funds are spent. Grant writing and allocation of money would be done from an office in Juneau. The tribe would be sovereign in name, but would lose the power to situate decision-making within 'unofficial' local law.

Law, whether it is 'official' legal law or 'unofficial' local law, creates the conditions of culture (Weisbrod 2002: 2). Legal rules with a narrow focus are prioritized in the corporate, incorporated, legislative and enforcement style of government. Those who understand law as "a system of precise rules for assessing responsibility and reject as irrelevant everything that is not circumscribed within these rules" fare better in the corporate, legislative Euro-American legal system (Conley and O'Barr 1990: 58-59). Narrow rule orientation is more typical of people who work in the Euro-American public and business sphere, the sphere from which legal rules are most often created.

In contrast, most people from Keex' Kwaan are oriented toward relationships, the stories behind stories, and the 'unofficial' day-to-day laws of community. Regionalizing tribal decision-making about justice and social programs would increase the divide between Keex' Kwaan 'local' laws and 'official' laws. It would further divide leadership. Without strong, cooperative and respected leadership, Keex' Kwaan's ability to solve its own problems diminishes. Regionalization through borough governments would exacerbates a similar divide between community and leadership in Keex' Kwaan.

Considering that Euro-American legal processes are an aspect of the leadership divisions in Keex' Kwaan, how might local people be empowered if 'unofficial' Tlingit laws were more consciously recognized and included in the legal decision-making of the tribal corporation, the city council and the IRA tribal board? How might such community-sensitive practices allow for and encourage leadership cooperation between these three entities? With greater recognition of the value of 'unofficial' laws, could the three legal entities find ways to combine their decision-making efforts through community-wide meetings? How might such processes acknowledge community consensus, family loyalty, leadership that includes respected elders, and Tlingit laws concerning respect for the environment? Ultimately, what could representatives of 'official' state and federal legal institutions learn about the systems they serve by letting go and encouraging Keex' Kwaan to re-evaluate its legal practices? What might the 'state' and the 'nation' learn about the possibilities of legal pluralism by supporting Keex' Kwaan in rebuilding respect for local leadership through engaging more closely with the day-to-day processes of 'unofficial' Tlingit law?

# References

BOURDIEU, Pierre
1991    *Language and Symbolic Power.* John B. Thompson (ed.). Cambridge, Mass.: Harvard University.
CONLEY, John M. and William M. O'BARR
1990    *Rules Versus Relationships: The Ethnography of Legal Discourse.* Chicago: The University of Chicago Press.
DOCHERTY, Jayne Seminare
2004    'Power in the social/political realm.' *Marquette Law Review.* 87: 862-866.
FERNANDEZ, James and Mary Taylor HUBER (eds.)
2001    'Introduction.' In *Irony in Action: Anthropology, Practice, and the Moral Imagination.* Chicago: The University of Chicago Press.
GAVENTA, John
1982    *Power and Powerlessness: Quiescence and Rebellion in an Appalachian Valley.* University of Illinois Press.
HARRISON, Dale
2003    Transcript of two interviews with US Senator Ted Stevens on Alaska Public Radio News. Oct. 3.
HOWARTH, David and Yannis STAVRAKAKIS
2000    'Introducing discourse theory and political analysis.' Pp. 1-23 in David Howarth, Alletta J. Norval, and Yannis Stavrakakis (eds.), *Discourse theory and political analysis: Identities, hegemonies and social change.* Manchester and New York: Manchester University Press.

JACKSON, Dawn.

2002    Letter to the Ford Foundation Community Forestry Research Workshop. Jackson, Mike

JACKSON, Mike

2005    Correspondence with Kathryn Fulton. November.

JOHNSON, Charles

2000    *Heritage: Keex' Kwaan – A Conspectus.* OVK Archives. Kake, *Alaska.*

LACLAU, E.

1989    *New Reflections on the Revolution of Our Time.* London: *Verso.*

MITCHELL, Donald

1997    *Sold America: The Story of Alaska Natives and their Land, 1867-1959.* Dartmouth College: University Press of New England.

NORVAL, Aletta

1997    'Frontiers in question.' *Acta Philosophica:* 51-76.

TIE, Warwick

1999    *Legal Pluralism: Toward a Multicultural Conception of Law.* Dartmouth: Ashgate.

WALZER, Michael

1992    *What it Means to be an American: Essays on the American Experience.* New York: Marsilio.

WEISBROD, Carol

2002    *Emblems of Pluralism: Cultural Differences and the State.* Princeton: Princeton University Press.

WITTEVEEN, Willem

1998    'Significant, symbolic and symphonic laws.' Pp. 27-70 in Hanneke van Schooten (ed.), *Semiotics and Legislation: Jurisprudential, Institutional and Sociological Perspectives.* Liverpool UK: Deborah Charles Publications.

WORL, Rosita

1999    *Tlingit At.oow: Tangible and Intangible Property.* Thesis. Cambridge: Harvard University.

# COMMUNITY RIGHTS AND STATUTORY LAWS: POLITICS OF FOREST USE IN UTTRAKHAND HIMALAYAS

Pampa Mukherjee

> Forests are all gone now. There used to be thick growth of Sal and Oak when I came to this village as a young bride. I am seventy years now. In fifty years I have seen everything change. I see more guards and officials now rather than trees. The government is there not to improve our condition but to win elections. (Rukmini Devi, Bhansali village, Nainital)

In many parts of Uttranchal, the newly created hill state of India, one finds numerous accounts like Rukmini Devi's. For the rural *pahari*[1] community the formation of this new political entity is yet to make a substantive difference to their everyday lives and to the state of forests around them. In fact many of them enumerate incidences of conflict that the villagers have had with the state while asserting their customary claim on forest resources. Few lament that, once a composite entity, the forest is now being fragmented and has been demarcated into diverse property regime types such as reserved and village( *panchayat* forests. The existence of multiple property regimes and conflicting rules and regulations has made the relationship between the people, state and forest a contested domain.

Given the above context, the present paper aims to highlight the dominance of statutory laws over local self-governing institutions and how community space is

---

[1] The term *pahari* implies hill people.

constricted in the name of participatory governance. It argues that, while for both national government and international donor agencies democratic decentralization has become a major concern, in implementing their programs at the field level they tend to treat communities as mere beneficiaries rather than as active partners. It also highlights the fact that the introduction of New Joint Forest Management in 1996 has overridden the customary claims of communities on forests practiced over decades. Further, it shows how boundaries and fences have become sites of anxiety, creating artificial enclaves and plots, and in the process excluding communities from their rightful access to resources. The present paper, which is based on extensive field research in the Nainital district of Uttranchal, draws its insights from in-depth interviews with local residents.

## The Field

Uttranchal was formed in 2001. Historically the area has been witness to a series of social movements. The famous *chipko* movement spearheaded by the women of the region is one the finest examples of environmental movements in India. Administratively the region has thirteen districts.

Agriculture is the predominant economic activity and three quarters of the land holdings belong to sub-marginal or marginal categories of farmers, with an average of 0.37 hectare of land each. Land distribution is relatively equal, cases of land holdings of over 2 hectares being rare, and landlessness low. The area's agro-pastoral economy is still predominantly subsistence-based, with about 50% of rural households, including the rural elite, having a high dependence on village commons and forest lands. Moreover, the level of urbanization is extremely low in most districts, thus ruling out significant industrial or service activity, and hence a large portion of the population is dependent on forests for economic sustenance. Lack of employment has led to a high male out-migration in search of employment, which makes the women left behind effectively managers of the rural household economy

Forests constitute a significant portion of the landuse map of Uttranchal, covering 60% of the total geographical area. It is the fourth most forested state in India. Forests are a source of livelihood for rural residents and provide resources such as fodder, fuel, green manure, and construction timber which are critical to the household economy. In their absence, effective household incomes would decline substantially. In such a context, the process of determining how forests can be collectively and appropriately managed is vitally important. It may be mentioned here that forest in Uttranchal is managed by different administrative agencies, with three different categories of forest land for this purpose:

Forests under the Forest Department;
*Panchayati* or Community Forests under *Van Panchayats* (Forest
      Councils); and
Forests under the Revenue Department.

Of the total forest area two-thirds are under the jurisdiction of the Forest Department. Of the 34,000 sq km, 30,000 sq km (88%) are under the jurisdiction of government and only 4,000 sq km (12%) are managed by *Van Panchayats* or the forest councils.

In Uttranchal, though there exist different property regimes like state, common and private, such distinctions are primarily on paper and Gururani argues that they are quite ambiguous in everyday practice as there may be overlapping of property types (Gururani 2000: 172). However the local residents can clearly identify different forest types in the region under study, which, apart from their local knowledge of the landscape, is also the result of the strong enforcement of boundary rules and regulations by the forest department to demarcate *reserved forests* from community as well as civil/*soyam* lands which are under the revenue department. *Van Panchayats* have however their own set of working rules concerning forest use.[2] They may vary depending upon the local conditions and requirements and as these rules are collectively evolved, they are binding on all members of the village/villages sharing[3] a forest patch. It is thus apparent that there exist more than one set of rules and codes of property. It is interesting to note that despite having codified and elaborate rules defined through statutory laws for *reserved forests*, there are numerous instances of 'rule violation' as villagers tend not only to access but also to extract non-timber forest products like fuel and fodder from government-owned forest lands. In fact in their collective memories the collection of fuel and fodder are their customary rights, and this co-existence of plural laws creates conditions and relations that permit use, access and

---

[2] In the area under study one can identify four sets of working rules, which can be classified under use, monitor, sanction and arbitration.

[3] A village forest may be shared by one or more villages depending upon the proximity to each other and the area of forest demarcated as *panchayati* forest.

abstraction of products from the forest in the region. Apart from statutory laws defining governance of forests there are also "deeply embedded cultural, historical and economic claims that allows rules and codes of property to be redefined and reinterpreted outside their narrow legal confines" (Gururani 2000).

## *Van Panchayats*

*Van Panchayats* or Forest Councils are considered unique examples of the decentralized governance of natural resources in Uttranchal. They were an outcome of conflicts and compromises that followed the settlements and reservations of forests in the hills in the first part of the last century. The first government-approved *Van Panchayat* was formed in 1931. According to recent estimates (2001), there are about 6777 Van Panchayats in Uttaranchal. These *Van Panchayats* manage a forest area of about four thousand square kilometers forming about 12% of the total forest area of the state. It may be observed that *Van Panchayats* are present only in the hill-districts. Haridwar and Udhamsingh Nagar districts located in the foothills and *Terai* region do not have any *Van Panchayats*.

It may be mentioned here that community forest managed in accordance with the Van Panchayat Act is a hybrid of state ownership and community responsibility. In managing and controlling community forest use Forest Councils are guided by rules laid down by the Revenue Department and by the technical advice of the Forest Department. In contrast to civil forests, community forests or *Panchayati* forests as they are popularly known are not 'open' forests. As has already been mentioned, access to and use of forests are guided by a set of working rules meticulously designed and implemented by the communities. Four identifiable sets of working rules exist relating to Use, Monitoring, Sanctions and Arbitration. Though only notionally or nominally owned by the communities, community forests are in a very real sense common property with an identifiable user group, have finite subtractive benefits and are susceptible to degradation when used beyond a sustainable limit. However what is more important is that the local users consider them as their collective property and in a real sense they are not actually divisible. These forests are nevertheless not completely immune from misuse, and their condition varies from poor to very good.

The Forest Council Act prescribes how *Panchayats* can be formed and imposes duties on village *Panchayats*. The objective is to protect the forest areas and ensure that forest products are being distributed among the entitled holders in an equitable manner. Kumaun Panchayat Forest Rules enacted under section 28(2) of the Indian Forest Act 1927 provide broad guidelines for the supervision and management of forests under the control of *Van Panchayats*. These Forest Council rules lay down the broad parameters of management practices to be followed by the *Van Panchayats*.

The main functions of *Van Panchayats* are as follows:

(a)     To develop and protect forests by preventing indiscriminate felling of trees and to fell only those which are marked by the Forest Department and are useful from the point of view of silviculture.

(b)     To ensure that there is no encroachment on *Van Panchayati* land, and that no rules enacted under the Kumaon and Sodic Land Act of 1948 are violated and that no land is encroached upon for agricultural purposes without prior permission.

(c)     To construct and fix boundary pillars and to maintain them (Forest Rules 18(c)).

(d)     To carry out the directives of the Sub-Divisional Magistrate in developing and protecting forests (Forest Rules 18(a)).

(e)     To distribute its produce amongst entitled holders in an equitable manner (Forest Rules 18 (e)).

(f)     To close 20% of the area of the forest for grazing every year.

They have the following punitive powers:

(a)     To levy fines up to Rs. 50 with the prior approval of the Deputy Commissioner (later revised to Rs. 500).

(b)     To seize intruding cattle and impound them under the Cattle Trespass Act of 1871.

(c)     To forfeit the weapons of the offender.

They have the following administrative and financial powers:

(a)     To sell grass, fallen twigs and stone slates to local people.

(b)     To auction trees up to the value of Rs.5000 with the approval of the District Magistrate and Divisional Forest Officer. Auctioning of trees above Rs. 5000 is done by the Forest Department.

(c)     To distribute the income realized from resin, timber and fees. This is to be distributed as follows:

(i)    *zilla parishad* is given 20% for creating and maintaining infrastructure;

(ii)   *gaon sabha* is given 40% for local development schemes if approved by the Block Development Committee;

(iii)  the remainder is to be ploughed back by the Forest Department for maintenance and development of *Panchayat* rules.

The villagers feel that, through the Act, the bureaucracy exercises excessive control over Forest *Panchayats*. Bureaucrats on the other hand believe that, in the absence of central control, villagers would clear fell the entire forest (Personal Communcation 2002). Nonetheless on analyzing the rules it becomes quite clear that they, while making the *Panchayats* responsible for proper management of the forests, deny them the necessary powers, which seem rather to be vested in the revenue and forest officials. For instance in section 17 of the 1976 Act it is stated that, before a watchman or any other paid staff is employed by the *Panchayat*, previous approval of the Deputy Commissioner (DC) is necessary. An offence involving a sum of Rs. 50/- can be compounded only with the previous approval of the DC. Similarly permission is required if seized property (stolen timber, etc.) is proposed to be sold. Administrative control over the *Panchayat* thus still lies with the DC, and technical control has been given to the Forest Department.


## Traditional Institutions and Contemporary Challenges

As has been mentioned above, the formal legal rules that have taken prominence in recent years have eroded the element of trust and cooperation among villagers in the use of land and access to forest resources. In this context the most significant effect is the manner in which the institution of the *Van Panchayat* has been affected. The importance and effectiveness of institutions like *Van Panchayats* lay in the fact that the 'social boundaries' which they evolved and constructed, and consequently the working rules that they devised to ensure optimal, efficient use of resources, were primarily through people's involvement and general consent. This gave these institutions a certain amount of credibility and legitimacy. However over the years there has been a steady decline of the democratic and participatory space which these village level institutions provide to their members. Unfortunately the Forest Department's tendency to monitor the functioning of these institutions through generalized rules and regulations in the name of 'participatory governance' has crippled these institutions, reducing them and the communities to the level of mere implementers or at best non-official managers with no substantial powers. The introduction of Joint Forest Management in the region in 1997 can be interpreted as an initiative which tends to create artificial boundaries by "crafting administrative communities for better governance, self sufficiency and cost-management" (Agrawal 2001).

Though the *Van Panchayats* managed to survive these multiple obstacles and challenges to their authority in many villages, they have been faced with two additional crises in the last few years which may have long term implications i.e. they may either weaken them or bring about their demise as relatively democratic and self-governing forest management institutions. Ironically, these new threats are primarily new initiatives that are being promoted in the name of 'participatory governance' or 'state-people partnership' in managing natural resources. The rapid formation of new *Van Panchayats* under the direction of the Revenue Department; and the introduction of 'Village Forest Joint Management' by the Forest Department are two such initiatives and Sarin points out that in reality they are basically an attempt to transfer more authority to the state at the expense of communities.

*New* Van Panchayats

Until recently *Van Panchayats* were primarily local initiatives, created out of genuine concern of the people to protect their forest, which culturally is their provider and protector. However a recent spurt in the creation of *Van Panchayats*, coinciding with the inflow of vast funds in the state for JFM (Joint Forest Management) activity has created new sets of complexity for these self-governing institutions. There has been an increase in the demarcation of remaining civil lands as village forests. For example, in Nainital district there were only 61 *Van Panchayats* at the time of independence, but this number had increased to 495 by 1999 (Sarin 2001). The formation of these institutions, which was need-based and demand-driven, has been converted into a supply-driven one. Instead of the villagers collectively applying for a village forest, the administration has imposed its decisions, irrespective of whether *Panchayats* are required or not. It also ignores other issues such as ongoing boundary disputes, and existing community management arrangements.

Earlier, a *Van Panchayat* could cover more than two or more revenue villages. With the coming of new policy which requires a separate *Van Panchayat* for every revenue village internal cohesion, cooperation and trust among users has been disrupted. Moreover some multi-village *Van Panchayats* have been re-organized in an abrupt and authoritative manner without consulting the local villagers, disrupting thereby the internal social adjustments and exacerbating intra- and inter-village conflicts. Traditionally, villagers had developed an effective multi-village governance system that was both democratic and equitable. Reorganization of *Van Panchayats* has in fact destroyed the traditional culture of resource sharing. According to earlier practices *Van Panchayats* were formed taking into consideration a number of factors and one of them was the topography and the forest cover, particularly in those cases where the institution was shared by multiple villages. The present abrupt division of forest councils allowed neither the forest area nor the species composition to be evenly distributed among the villages, and unequal distribution has resulted. Some are now left with small forest patches with only Chir pine, while others have all the fodder bearing areas, which again has created bitterness among villages and encouraged conflict rather than catalysing cooperation. The changes have also failed to address any of the major problems plaguing the existing *Van Panchayats* – the lack of effective and easily accessible dispute resolution mechanisms, inter-village inequity in the availability of forest areas, the erosion of *Panchayat* authority, and the limited control over forest-based livelihoods and income. The rapid and abrupt formation of *Van Panchayats*, rather than expanding space for local forest management, seems to have reduced it further. According to a study carried out by the Rural Litigation and Entitlement *Kendra* (RLEK) in Uttranchal, the recent increase in government interference has resulted in *Van Panchayats* losing their original character. The interference by the forest department into the functioning of *Van Panchayats* is "fast eroding the spirit of forest conservation by the local communities". It is too early to predict the effects that state-driven *Van Panchayat* formation might have on local livelihoods, social relations and forest management practices. The process of their formation, however, gives reason for concern.

*Village Forest Joint Management (VFJM)*

VFJM, which was introduced by the Forest Department in Uttranchal in 1997, is not only problematic but also paradoxical as it strengthens state control rather than expanding democratic space, by curtailing people's traditional rights. Unlike Joint Forest Management (JFM) in other states which enables villagers to participate in the management of forest lands under the Forest Department's jurisdiction, in Uttranchal the VFJM Rules enable the department to become the dominant partner in the management of *Van Panchayats* and civil forest lands. Moreover the land being brought under VFJM falls under the jurisdiction of *Van Panchayats* or the Revenue department and not of the Forest Department. The land is managed in collaboration with *Gram Sabhas*, the democratic institutions of local self-government at the lowest level.

According to VFJM Rules, Village Forest Committees (VFCs) may be formed where there are no *Van Panchayats* and there is an effort to link VFJM with local self-government through *Gram Sabhas*. VFCs are expected to be representative of key local interests, with one seat each designated for women, scheduled castes/tribes, backward castes, and for persons with a particular interest in forests. The head of the *Gram Sabha* is the President of the VFC and the forest guards are its member secretary, the two also jointly holding the committee's account. As *Gram Sabhas* in the hills cover more than one village, it is possible that neither the president nor the secretary of the VFC may be a resident of the village whose forest management institution they head. Whereas linking community forest management institutions with those of local government is highly desirable, the order for constituting VFC is a top down, mechanical prescription. It says nothing about strengthening participatory governance by the *Gram Sabhas* and forest committees or their respective roles and responsibilities within the local governance structure.

While 'communities' have come to occupy center stage in most of the discourse on development and participation, they in fact tend to become targets or victims of development projects, whether it is the construction of dams, the creation of parks and protected areas or projects like *JFMs*.It may be pointed out that creation of *VFC*s emphasizing participatory governance of forests was not an outcome of any demand of the people in this hill state but was one of the conditionalities of the World Bank's $65m loan given to the Uttar Pradesh Forestry Project for the period 1998-2002 (Sarin 2001). As a necessary fallout of agreements between the State Government and the World Bank, *JFM* received priority in the region, which in fact accounted for 30% of the total budget. Ironically enough the Bank's appraisal documents do not state any substantive reason for promoting *JFM* and neither does it specify any process to ensure participation of different stakeholders in *VJFM*. In the absence of any knowledge, experience and mechanism available to the Bank to motivate 'participation', the responsibility for framing them rests with the Forest Department with no history or experience of working with *Van Panchayats* or knowledge of how to facilitate 'participatory governance'. Experienced and long standing *Van Panchayats* with an adequate institutional history along with other Non-Governmental/ Civil Society Organizations working in the same sector would have the best alternative but they are distinctively conspicuous by their absence.

*Van Panchayats* and other community institutions are treated as the objects of attention, rather than active participants in redefining their future destiny. The World Bank project simply assumes the desirability of importing the standard JFM model from other states into Uttranchal, with all its shortcomings, instead of exporting a strengthened *Van Panchayats* framework to them. In fact most of the Non governmental organizations functioning in this newly formed state demand that Uttaranchal government should not accept World Bank liabilities taken by the UP government in the name of JFM, Eco-Development and Watershed management.

Though it is too early to see the impacts of VJFM on forest based livelihoods and forest quality, the content of the VFJM Rules suggests a loss of democratic space for local villagers. Despite claims to empower local forest users, the rules do much to achieve the opposite, by instituting control over decision-making and thus creating dependence with no control over forest resources. This fact becomes all the more conspicuous if one looks at the formation of Committees and selection of villages to be brought under VFJM. Prioritization and selection of villages for VFJM is done by the Forest Department in accordance with several selection criteria, making it a supply, rather than a demand driven process. 'Spearhead teams' communicate with and develop microplans for selected villages. These teams consist of one ACF; one ranger or deputy ranger; one forester or forest guard; and two NGO 'social motivators'. Experienced *Van Panchayat* leaders with decades of experience of community forest management have no role as facilitators and technical advisors. Instead they are being motivated to protect forests. The agreement to be signed by the participating villagers refers to them as beneficiaries rather than as equal partners. The discourse, vocabulary and the content of the policy, being highly patronizing, encourages hierarchy among stakeholders and managers and thereby reduces the community forests to mere administrative zones (Gururani 2000).

Given the circumstances there is a great apprehension that the taking over of forest management by the Forest Department and its intrusion into the functioning of the *Van Panchayats* will fast erode the spirit of forest conservation by the local communities. It represents another example of the total disregard by the State of traditional, community-run systems of natural resource management in the region.

## Conclusion

This paper therefore argues that the mere implementation of policies is not sufficient to ensure a truly democratic participatory space. The process has to be need based and evolved rather than being imposed and given. Though democratic decentralization is frequently initiated as a precondition to participatory development, such participation will be merely passive if the decentralization process fails to consider the ecological, social, cultural and institutional specificities of a given society. Further participatory governance can have democratic relevance only if 'communities' are brought to the centre stage of decision-making. It will then become necessary to recognize, accept and treat communities as relevant actors rather than mere recipients in using, managing and governing resources. At the same time it is important to understand what are the implications of bringing the community back into the development discourse.

*Van Panchayats,* despite being an excellent example of state-people partnership which has been relatively successful in managing forest resources in the region, are facing challenges from unrealistic and target-driven policies which are likely to affect its democratic functioning. There is a need to replicate such institutions in other areas rather than interfering with those which already exist. Moreover, Non-Governmental Organizations need to play more active roles in keeping these institutions alive by bringing the communities to the centre stage of decision-making. In order to strengthen such community-oriented institutions, it is necessary to identify such similar institutions and undertake comparative studies on them so that any anomalies which may be found can be removed.

## References

AGARWAL, C.
1996    'Boundary and property rights in Uttarakhand forests.' *Wasteland News,*
        February-April. New Delhi: Society for Promotion of Wasteland
        development.
AGRAWAL, Arun
2001    'State formation in community spaces? Decentralization of control over
        forests in the Kumaon Himalayas, India.' *Journal of Asian Studies*

AGRAWAL, R.
1999      'Van Panchayats in Uttrakhand: A Case Study.' *Economic and Political Weekly*, September 25.

ARNOLD, J.E.M. and W.C. STEWART
1991      *Common Property Resource Management in India,* Tropical Forestry Papers 24. Oxford: Oxford Forestry Institute.

BALLABH, V. and K. SINGH
1988      *Van (Forest) Panchayats in Uttar Pradesh Hills: A Critical Analysis,* Research Paper No.2. Anand.India: Institute of Rural Management.

BANDOPADHYAY, J. and V. SHIVA,
1988      'Political economy of ecological movement.' *Economic and Political Weekly* June 11: 1223-1332.

FEENY, David
1988      The Demand for and Supply of Institutional Arrangements". In Vincent Ostrom, David Feeny and H. Picht (eds.), *Rethinking Institutional Analysis and Development.* San Francisco: ICS Press.

GUHA, Ramchandra
1989      The *Unquiet Woods: Ecological Change and Peasant Resistance in the Himalaya.* New Delhi: Oxford University Press.

GURURANI, S,
2000      'Regimes of control, strategies of access: politics of forest use in Uttarakhand, Himalaya, India.' Pp70-190 in A. Agrawal and K. Sivaramakrishnan (eds.), *Agrarian Environments, Resources, Representations, Rule in India.* London and Durham: Duke University Press.

POFFENBERGER, Mark and B. McGEAN (eds.)
1996      *Village Voices and Forest Choices: Joint Forest Management in India.* Delhi: Oxford University Press.

SARIN, M
2001      'Disempowerment in the name of participatory forestry? Village Forest Joint Management in Uttarakhand.' *Forest, Trees and People*, Newsletter 44, April.

# BOOK REVIEW

Prakash Shah, *Legal Pluralism in Conflict: Coping with Cultural Diversity in Law*. London, Sydney, Portland Oregon: Glass House Press. 2005.

Gordon R. Woodman

The main thesis of this book states that the legal pluralism of Britain has been intensified, and the conflict it engenders has been increased, by the immigration from outside Europe which has taken place since World War II; and that in these circumstances the state law fails woefully to treat ethnic minorities fairly, omitting to understand and recognize their laws. This thesis is developed primarily with regard to the post-war history of immigration and nationality law, Dr Shah's main fields of expertise. But he also has much of interest to say concerning the teaching about ethnic minorities in law schools (or the absence of such teaching), the treatment of issues arising from cultural diversity in homicide cases, and many other issues pertinent to the main thesis. These fields have been neglected by legal writers, and this work must be welcomed.

Arguing for his first premise, that legal pluralism arising from cultural diversity is today a major feature of the legal scene in Britain, the author adopts the analyses of legal pluralism presented by Masaji Chiba (Chapter 1, referring to Chiba 1989, 1998). Chiba proposed inter alia that "the fundamental structure of the working whole of law" in human society should be seen as having a three-level structure, consisting of official law, unofficial law, and legal postulate (Chiba 1989: 138-40). The first, official law is usually state law. Secondly, unofficial law is "authorized in practice by the general consensus of a certain circle of people, whether of a country or within or beyond it" (Chiba 1989: 139). The notion includes the normative orders of the communities with which Shah is concerned, being the "self conscious and more or less well organised communities entertaining and living by their own different systems of beliefs and practices" (p. 1, quoting Parekh 2000). Clearly, if these orders are recognized as a category of law, there is a marked degree of legal pluralism in Britain today. Thirdly, "the legal postulate of a country is the foundation of its official and unofficial law which it also justifies and orients" (Chiba 1989: 140). This is later referred to by Chiba as the "identity postulate" of "the working whole structure of law of a people" (Chiba 1989: Chaps. 11, 12).

Shah's book may be seen as making the case for a particular type of identity postulate of British law, He states:

> This study takes inspiration from Chiba's argument that it is essential to observe conflicts within legal pluralism, the better thereby to highlight and to manage them 'wisely', and to address this from the subjective perspective of the recipient of legal pluralism (p. 9).

The case for an identity postulate which will manage conflicts wisely is advanced through detailed studies of the ways in which current state law responds to situations in which human activity has been influenced by the norms of ethnic minority laws. Of a succession of such cases Shah argues that British legal thinking is strongly ethnocentric, showing little understanding of and no interest in cultures other than that of the white majority, indigenous population. The dominant view adheres to legal centralism, the belief that "law is and should be the law of the state, uniform for all persons, exclusive of all other law, and administered by a single set of state institutions" (Griffiths 1986: 3).

Shah makes a powerful case, although in places he seems unduly dismissive of those with whom he disagrees. For example he regards it as "incredible" that the Court of Appeal upheld a decision despite his own published comment on it, "three senior judges apparently unable to see the, by this stage, ridiculous position the legal proceedings had reached" (p. 134). However, generally he presents a convincing critique of the recent development of immigration and nationality law. Especially telling, in the view of this reviewer, are his accounts of the persistent findings that the laws observed in resident ethnic minority communities can be recognised only as 'foreign' laws (pp. 34-35). The consequence has been that the only ground for applying laws claimed to be the personal laws of members of these groups in state courts has been the recognition of these laws as foreign systems of law applicable according to the rules of private international law (p. 101).

One may wonder whether British state law has always rejected the recognition of other laws so inflexibly as Shah suggests. While there has historically always been a centralising, homogenising tendency in the common law, there has also been a long tradition of abstaining from intervening when minorities apply their own laws within their own communities. The large body of case-law on the recognition and enforcement of local customs suggests that these were seen as a significant element in the common law for centuries until industrialisation and urbanisation eroded their social effectiveness. The history of Jewish law in England shows a similar approach. After their readmission to England around 1660, the Jewish community established their own places of worship, celebrated their own religious forms of marriage, and generally regulated relations within their community. It has been said that they had their own "miniature republics, with councils and law courts of their own" (Kiernan 1978: 26). Only in the 19th century were Jewish marriages brought within the general English law regulating the incidents of marriage and the processes of its termination. Again, the Huguenots, protestants who in the 16th and 17th centuries took refuge in England from religious persecution in France, generally created their own church and work environment, and the elaborate organization of their churches effectively regulated the lives of members of this community (Gwynn 1985; also Kiernan 1978: 38-39). Huguenots were eventually, in the 18th century, assimilated into the majority English community. Jews, with individual exceptions, were only partially assimilated. Cases such as these need to be studied further.

That part of British legal history concerned with the acquisition of colonies and government of colonized peoples displays readiness on the part of the state to recognize personal laws. The notion of personal law was the basis for the diffusion of English law through British settlers who "brought their law with them". But was equally the basis for the principle that the existing laws of colonized peoples continued to apply to them after British sovereignty had been established, and were to be observed and enforced by British colonial courts. (The law is conveniently summarized by Roberts-Wray 1966: 539-44.) Shah draws a neat analogy between the transplantation of the common law through settlement by groups of British and the transplantation of the laws of ethnic minorities through their immigration to Britain (pp. 4, 60). The fact that the diffusion of the common law was aided and accompanied by a firm recognition of the principle of personal law raises questions about the legal foundation for the current reluctance to recognize personal laws within Britain.

Shah recognizes that much more work needs to be done in this field, and explains that the book "emerges out of a perceived urgency to provide students with accessible material and to continue the debate among the wider communities of ethnic minorities, scholars, policy makers, legal professionals and others..." (p. 26). It may be suggested that there is an urgency to add to the debate some other information and arguments.

There is a need to consider seriously the considerable volume of literature which debates the possibility that there are universal values against which all laws, including the unofficial laws of ethnic communities as well as state laws can be assessed. Most of us would recognize that it is not entirely coherent to assert a strong moral relativism while also criticizing the actions of a state and its judiciary on moral grounds. There is in Shah's book no discussion of, nor even reference to the debates about group rights (e.g. Kymlicka 1995, 2001). The Foreward by Roger Cotterrell, suggesting that liberal individualism as a practical attitude has become "socially ignorant and ethically barren" (p. ix) points in this direction, but the possibility is not pursued. In consequence criticism, for example, of the practice of polygamy, permitted in the laws of origin of some minority communities, tends to be dismissed as ethnocentric and assimilationist. The vast literature on human rights, much of which is relevant to the issues discussed in this book, is dismissed as also ethnocentric, or is ignored at points where it might have been relevant (Chap. 5). The criticisms directed at Poulter (1998), to the effect that his judgements were affected by an adherence to legal centralism (e.g. pp. 35-36) are in general well taken, but more consideration might have been given to the possibility that there was strength in some of his evaluative arguments.

It is also unfortunate, since Shah devotes a chapter to the culture defence (Chap. 4, on homicide), that he does not take account of Renteln (2004), which presents a huge volume of information and argumentation on the subject. Although Renteln writes primarily about the USA, her book contains many examples from other countries. Moreover, the USA is the country in which the topic appears most frequently to have arisen, and there are many possibilities of fruitful comparison with Britain. Renteln also contains reports arising from applications to present in state courts evidence of the cultures of minority communities. Much of this could have been relevant to the chapter on expert opinions on South Asian laws in immigration cases (Chap. 7.

The discussion does not often move beyond critique of past and present events and policies to analyze the field more generally and present proposals for the future. If ethnic laws are to receive recognition in British state law, some pressing practical problems will arise. It will be necessary to formulate principles determining how a 'community' is to be identified, and also to define the scope of a 'law'. Many members of minority groups observe or use their laws for some purposes, but not for other parts of their lives. These somewhat indeterminate 'communities' have often changed and adapted their laws of origin to meet the circumstances of life in Britain. If a policy of recognition of these laws is accepted, it will be necessary not only to determine the content of the social norms which are observed in practice by members of minority communities, but also to find criteria to distinguish between those norms which are to be classed as legal, and those which are not. It will be necessary to decide to what extent there is to be normative recognition (in which the institutions of the recognizing law adopt norms from the recognized law), and to what extent institutional recognition (in which the recognizing law cedes jurisdiction to institutions of the recognized law). There is much colonial experience of both forms which may throw light on these issues. Normative recognition may be more acceptable, but it requires law-makers to confront the problem that institutions, such as courts, which recognize norms require reliable sources of information as to their content (and will almost certainly make errors in this respect); and that they often cannot as a practical matter enforce, through their mechanisms, the norms of a system with widely different concepts and practices from their own. Shah discusses well the difficulty which state judges experience in trying to ascertain and understand non-state laws. He does not mention the necessity to adapt practiced non-state laws to enable them to operate as lawyers' customary law in the state law system.

Finally, it must be questioned how far Shah succeeds in his aim of adopting a "subjective perspective". (A well-considered argument for this perspective is contained in Vanderlinden (1989, 1993).) Anthropologists specialize in this. Lawyers, including legal academics, are with a few exceptions quite unequipped for it. In consequence our efforts to improve the general legal situation seem always to result in recommendations for legal action by state law alone. Chiba's notion of a legal postulate is the legal postulate of a 'country', a state. So in developing the identity postulate Shah can seek only to establish a formal recognition of legal pluralism by state law. The result will be state law pluralism (in which state law incorporates areas of non-state laws), not a conscious or planned deep legal pluralism, or legal pluralism in the strong sense as it is termed by Griffiths (1986), in which state law recognizes that it coexists with other, independently valid laws and vice versa. That mutual recognition of deep legal pluralism entails some adjustment within each law. Shah's final sentence reads:

It remains difficult to see the coexistence of these different orders [of the state and ethnic minorities] in harmony unless adjustments are made to *the official system* to make it more responsive to the socio-legal orders within its scope (p. 178, emphasis added).

A reasonably broad-minded legal centralist would not have put it very differently.

## References

CHIBA, Masaji
1989    *Legal Pluralism: Toward a General Theory through Japanese Legal Culture*, Tokyo: Tokai University Press.
1998    'Other phases of legal pluralism in the contemporary world.' *Ratio Juris* 11: 228-245.
GRIFFITHS, John
1986    'What is legal pluralism?' *Journal of Legal Pluralism* 14: 1-55.
GWYNN, Robin D.
1985    *Huguenot Heritage: The history and contribution of the Huguenots in Britain*. London: Routledge & Kegan Paul.
KIERNAN, V.G.
1978 "Britons Old and New", pp. 23-59 in Colin Holmes (ed.), *Immigrants and Minorities in British Society*, London: George Allen & Unwin, 1978.
KYMLICKA, Will (ed.),
1995    *The Rights of Minority Cultures*. Oxford: Oxford University Press.
2001    *Politics in the Vernacular: Nationalism, Multiculturalism, and Citizenship*. Oxford: Oxford University Press.
PAREKH, Bhikhu
2000    *Rethinking Multiculturalism: Cultural Diversity and Political Theory*. Basingstoke: Palgrave.
RENTELN, Alison Dundes
2004    *The Cultural Defense*. Oxford: Oxford University Press.
VANDERLINDEN, Jacques
1989    'Return to legal pluralism: twenty years later.' *Journal of Legal Pluralism* 28: 149-157.
1993    'Vers une nouvelle conception du pluralisme juridique.' *Revue de la recherche juridique - droit prospectif* XVIII: 573-583.